The Spark of God

THE SPARK
OF GOD

That You May Have Life Abundantly

James More-Molyneux
OBE DL

eagle

Guildford, Surrey

By the same author:
The Loseley Challenge, now available from the author
(London: Hodder & Stoughton, 1995)

British Library Cataloguing in Publication Data. A catalogue record for this book is available from the British Library.

Published by Eagle Publishing Ltd, PO Box 530, Guildford, Surrey GU2 4FH.

Typeset by Eagle
Printed by Cox & Wyman
ISBN No: 0 86347 371 7

Thomas Merton, in a crowded shopping centre in Louisville, Kentucky, recognised in a flash of joy the spark of God in each individual. There is a spark of God in every human being.

ACKNOWLEDGEMENTS

All who have helped, supported and put up with me during the period of writing, especially Sue.

Lizzie Cheriton-Sutton for transcribing my scrawl into typescript and Nicola Cheriton-Sutton and Christine West for their help.

Chilworth Friary and the Franciscan Brothers OFM for spiritual and material food and peace for writing. Fr Ignatius OFM for his inspirational assistance.

The Revd Pat Ashe for his encouragement and for the picture of Jesus during His earthly ministry.

Canon Anne Long for the voice of wisdom and experience.

CONTENTS

FOREWORD

James More-Molyneux and I were boyhood friends. We joined the same Regiment – the 4/7 Royal Dragoon Guards – in January 1941 and we both subsequently saw active service with Indian Cavalry regiments. It is not, I think, an exaggeration to say that by this experience I too was touched by 'the spark of God'.

Our Muslim, Hindu and Sikh troops never thought it 'odd' to discuss God in ordinary conversation without embarrassment and to call upon Him in times of trouble – or danger –. I regularly recall the words of one of our Tank Commanders in a moment of crisis 'Have faith in God, Sahib, he is a very reliable fellow!'

It is a myth to believe that Christianity is a religion of weakness or feebleness unworthy of strong men who like to picture themselves as masters of their own fate. The truth is the reverse. The people who crucified Christ never accused him of being weak – on the contrary they though of him as being too dynamic to be safe. It has been left to later generations to muffle our Lord's personality.

I believe with James More-Molyneux that it is our duty as Christians to display the same characteristics and to involve ourselves in today's problems both socially and politically. We politicians often talk about the importance of balance – of trade or industry, of payment, even of health – but there is another balance which is even more important – the balance in our lives between material progress and spiritual values.

This book brings this important balance into focus, written as it is by a man of action – a soldier, a pioneering farmer and also an enlightened and resourceful businessman.

Throughout his life James More-Molyneux, despite his material success, has never neglected the spiritual values of love and forgiveness and concern for the less fortunate – the very essence of Christianity.

The Rt Hon The Lord Weatherill DL
former Speaker of the House of Commons

INTRODUCTION

Writing a book is a chore. I learned that five years ago with
The Loseley Challenge, the story of Loseley, my company
Guildway and my Christian faith. On completion I
thankfully laid down my pen. I have a wonderful family and
friends and many interests and commitments. I am not a
theologian, scholar, bishop, priest or even lay reader. Why
on earth, in my eightieth year, should I write a book about
God? Sounds crazy and if I say that I have felt led to do so,
as with other things mentioned in the book, it also sounds
arrogant. Forgive me, but I do write in humility.

Not being an expert or professional, I am recording my
own personal thoughts and experiences. I have felt that I
should not discuss the contents with monks, clergy, experts,
friends or anyone else. This is merely a personal testimony
and I alone am responsible for the shortcomings. All too
aware of my many imperfections, I hope that sharing ways in
which I and others have found ourselves drawn closer to
God may be of help to someone.

There is another motivation for writing. The way we are
heading. Rapid material progress is being made, much of it
beneficial, particularly in the medical field. I am not a
'prophet of doom', but scientific and technical developments
are now taking place so rapidly that insufficient time is given
to consideration of possible side-effects. Remember DDT
and 'The Silent Spring', Chernobyl, the damaged Ozone
Layer, Acid Rain, pesticide poisoning and allergies, Nitrate
poisoning, now GM foods and cloning. One should perhaps
also consider nerve gases, germ warfare and the likes of

Saddam Hussein. Not alarmist, but facing facts; perhaps we should not bury our heads in the sand but raise them to Almighty God.

Just as much scientific progress has been good, so have we made great progress socially from the appalling conditions of poverty, misery and exploitation existing as recently as the Victorian era. I often think with horror of those farm workers being hanged for stealing a sheep to feed their starving family – or deported to Australia for poaching a rabbit, leaving their family with no support. There was terrible hardship, poverty and exploitation. The Church appears to have supported Authority more than the oppressed but individual Christians, such as Shaftesbury, dedicated themselves to changing these things, as did Wilberforce for the abolition of slavery.

Now in the Western world we are relatively affluent and the pursuit of personal wealth and enjoyment take precedence. For so many people God is now superseded, His teaching and commandments are ignored or forgotten. Sundays are for sport and shopping, 'Honour your father and mother' and 'Do not commit adultery' are not regarded as appropriate for our Times.

We all know about the appalling statistics on single-parent families, broken homes, child pregnancies, drug abuse . . . Turning away from God brings disaster, as the Israelites in the Old Testament so often discovered. We need to wake up to the facts before it is too late. Christina Rees recently gave an interesting sidelight on wealth and ambition in BBC Radio 4's *Thought For The Day*, reproduced with permission:

It's official: wealthy doesn't necessarily mean happy . . . Voluntary Service Overseas asked for research to be carried out because it has had an extraordinary two-thirds increase in applications from professional people in the past six months . . .

It transpires that the very things that these professionals had been chasing, namely, more money, more possessions and more status, were making them ill and miserable. Comparisons with the average person in Britain fifty years ago, show that we are indeed wealthier, but also ten times more likely to be depressed, forty times more likely to resort to violence and much more likely to have succumbed to alcoholism or drug abuse. Our gadgets and glamour are bought at the expense of our emotional well-being and mental health . . .

Hundreds of high-flyers are rediscovering some of the truth contained in Jesus' sermon on the mount on the folly of pursuing only the material.

What's been bothering these earners and spenders is the lack of a sense of fulfilment, purpose and identity, things that even a twice-a-year holiday in the sun, the latest car and designer labels don't seem able to give them. While it's clear that extreme poverty equals misery, and that even relative poverty creates problems, why is it that the complementary equation doesn't seem to work – that is, getting richer should make us happier or more fulfilled?

I think the equation poor-equals-miserable, rich-equals-happy, *would* balance if we inhabited only a material world, and if we were only material beings. But the world is a place of glorious paradox, and we are spirit as well as body, and our spirits become starved, neglected and restless when they are not fed and nourished.

That puts a clear case for a need for change of direction away from concentration on personal wealth, status and materialism. That we are 'spirit as well as body' is a fact still not understood by many good people, and will be covered in a later chapter.

The reaction to the emptiness of selfish materialism has begun and I am among those who believe that we may be on the verge of a great religious revival. Who has not heard of Alpha?

Chapter 1

IGNITING THE SPARK

I am aware of my good fortune in having been well kindled with Christian faith in early years. Many today do not have that benefit and have yet to find faith in God: it is to them that this chapter is dedicated.

Most people fail to find God because of complete misapprehensions. You may think: 'It is fine for him, he was probably brought up in a comfortable Christian home and went to church, but we had a tough childhood and never went near a church.' Here comes the good news. You are potentially higher in God's favour than I am. We have it on the authority of Jesus Himself. There is a whole chapter in the Bible devoted to this subject – Luke 15. First comes the parable of the owner of the hundred sheep, who leaves the ninety-nine to go and search for the lost sheep. 'In the same way, I tell you, there will be greater joy in Heaven over one sinner who repents than over ninety-nine righteous people who do not need to repent' (Luke 15:7). That is a clear message for all who doubt their worthiness and this message is repeated in the joy of the woman who finds her lost coin, and in the return home of the prodigal son who has squandered his inheritance in dissolute living. He received a joyous welcome from his father, who had the fatted calf killed in his honour, much to the resentment of his well-behaved brother, who had stayed at home, slaving for his father. These are clear messages of encouragement for those who believed themselves unworthy of God's forgiveness.

Is it worth the effort to find faith? If I did not think so, I would not have made the effort to write this book, so I hope that you will read on. Many people these days consider Christianity outdated, superseded by science, something just for those wanting to be monks, nuns or clergy. How wrong they are! Wrong also are people who believe that God excludes them because of their past misdeeds or non-belief.

Let us go back to the beginning. Jesus was in His prime during His years of ministry on earth and died at the age of thirty-four; most of His team were also young and very active. Although the Son of God, Jesus on earth was flesh and blood, born of woman, and, like us, subject to temptation, pain, tiredness and emotion. It helps to remember His human experience on earth and His ministry, the work that He did in miraculously healing and in teaching; we can relate to these and feel closer to Jesus. It is also of comfort to know, when we are going through bad times, that He can be with us to give us strength in our situation.

There are people who think of religion as something remote, irrelevant or complicated. Christianity should be none of these things; it is certainly not remote, for it is instantly available to everyone. The teaching of Jesus was above all about love, forgiveness and helping the poor and needy. All His teaching is relevant to us today. Being a Christian involves trying to live according to His will and His teaching. Very few could claim always to succeed, but through prayer we receive more strength. Jesus spent much time trying to escape the crowds in order to pray and we need to do the same. There is nothing remote or irrelevant in this. The more we try to follow the example and teaching of Jesus, the more relevant and practical we find it, especially when things are going wrong. In addition, we find strength through the greater depth that comes with our growing awareness of God's presence – this is something very real, which we can experience for ourselves.

Theologians do tend to make religion seem complicated to ordinary people. Fortunately we need not worry, for our Lord commended the humble and meek and the little children. We can be assured that it would not be His wish that our relationship with Him should be other than open and simple. Love and faith are the basis and the humble and meek will find faith more readily than the learned and arrogant, who require proof of every detail. God does so want us to find Him, to know Him and to love Him. Talking on this subject with a learned Franciscan friar, Father Ignatius OFM, he commented that God calls each one of us to share in His glories. He calls us personally, each in different ways, but in our secular society many individuals fail to be aware that God is calling them. We need to be open to receive Him. I can testify that it has happened to me, quite unexpectedly, as described later in this book.

There are so many positive reasons for believing in the existence of God. First is the reality of miracles. We start with the account in the New Testament of our Lord's miracles, mainly miracles of healing, with three people raised from the dead and many freed of evil spirits. Some will just not believe in miracles but it is a fact that, even after the crucifixion, resurrection and ascension of Jesus, His work was continued by the disciples and by Paul with vast numbers of people being healed of all their afflictions. As in our Lord's ministry people 'saw and believed and many were added to the believers'. It is a fact that the Church did grow and spread throughout the world and it certainly would not have done so if there had not been the evidence of power in the working of these miracles. All through the centuries there have been miraculous healings through prayer; these continue in our times on a daily basis all over the world and there are several examples recorded in the chapters of this book.

Angels do exist and many people have seen them, so presumably there must be a God to send and direct them. A number of books have been written recording the appearances of angels to people in a wide variety of situations, including times of bereavement and stress. A number of saintly people have miraculously received the sacred wounds of the cross, the stigmata, in their hands and feet. These include St Francis, who experienced in a vision Christ's anguish on the cross and His triumph over death. He received the wounds at the same time and they caused him considerable pain and embarrassment for the rest of his life. Dorothy Kerin, mentioned later in this book, is another who, in the twentieth century, received the stigmata.

Most Christians can give testimony to prayers that have been answered and there are many examples of guidance and discernment being received from God. Some of these are far too dramatic to be coincidences. The 'peace of God' described in this book is no ordinary peace; it comes from God and I can testify that it is deeper and more special than any other peace. The wonders of nature and the amazing creation which we call the human body surely point to a higher being and that is God.

Through the ages there have been the saints and martyrs and many holy men and women, each one of whom dedicated their life to God. Most of the martyrs were given the opportunity of being spared a horrendous death by torture if they renounced the name of Jesus. So deep was their belief in God that they preferred to be roasted alive, cut into small pieces, thrown to the lions as a spectacle for the nobles of Rome or to submit to any horrendous torture rather than deny Jesus Christ as Lord. That makes me feel very humble; just turning up at church on Sundays is rather inadequate by comparison. Yet there are many things that God has for each one of us to do and most of them demand some sacrifice. In the Old Testament we read that Abraham was prepared to sacrifice his son Isaac when he believed it to be God's will. Fortunately God, having tested Abraham's faith, intervened in time.

As indicated at the beginning of this chapter, my aim is to help the uncommitted to an awareness of the reality of the love and power of God, so that the spark can be kindled. It is important to believe in the scriptures and it helps to have corroboration of facts. Our revered Christian friends Pat and Marion Ashe have just handed me a fascinating account of how the American space programme proved the reality of two miracles recorded in the Old Testament. Although rather long, I feel it merits inclusion in full:

Mr Harold Hill, President of Curtis Engine Company, Maryland, consultant in the Space Programme relates: Astronauts and space scientists at Green Belt, Maryland were checking the position of the sun, moon and planets in space, where they would be one hundred years and one thousand years from now. We have to know this so we won't send a satellite up and have it bump into something later on in its orbits. They ran the computer measurement back and forth over the centuries and it came to a halt. The computer stopped and put up a red signal, which meant that there was something wrong either with the information fed into it or with the results as compared to the standards. They called in the service department to check it and they said: 'What's wrong?' Well, they found there is a day missing in space in elapsed time. They scratched their heads and tore their hair. There was no answer. Finally, a Christian said: 'I remember one time in Sunday School they talked about the sun standing still.' They said: 'Show us.' He got a Bible and went to the Book of Joshua where they found the Lord saying to Joshua: 'Fear them not, I have delivered them into thy

hand, there shall not a man of them stand before thee.'
Joshua was concerned because he was surrounded by
the enemy and if darkness fell they would overpower
them. So Joshua asked the Lord to make the sun stand
still! 'The sun stood still and the moon stayed and
hastened not to go down about a whole day.' The
astronauts and scientists said: 'There is the missing
day!' They checked the computers going back into the
time it was written and found it was close but not close
enough. The elapsed time that was missing back in
Joshua's day was twenty three hours and twenty
minutes – not a whole day. They checked the Bible and
there it was 'about (approximately) a day'. The word
'about' is important, but if you cannot account for
forty minutes you'll still be in trouble one thousand
years from now. Forty minutes had to be found because
it can be multiplied many times over in the orbits.

As the Christian thought about it, he remembered
somewhere in the Bible it said the sun went
BACKWARD. Scientists told him he was out of his
mind, but they got out the Book and read these words
in II Kings: Hezekiah, on his death-bed was visited by
the prophet Isaiah who told him that he was not going
to die. Hezekiah asked for a sign as proof. Isaiah said:
'Do you want the sun to go ahead ten degrees?'
Hezekiah said: 'It is nothing for the sun to go ahead ten
degrees, but let the shadow return backward ten
degrees.' Isaiah spoke to the Lord and the Lord brought
the shadow ten degrees BACKWARD! Ten degrees is
exactly forty minutes! Twenty-three hours and twenty
minutes in Joshua, plus forty minutes in II Kings make
the missing day in the universe! Isn't it amazing? Our
God is rubbing their noses in His truth!' (References:
Joshua 10:8 and 12, 13; II Kings 20:9–11)

Although, like many people, I normally read a small daily portion of the New Testament, I do not often read the Old Testament. If I had read those passages I would have accepted that the Lord did turn night into day for Joshua and also that He made the sun go backwards for Isaiah in order to impress King Hezekiah. Faith is very important and our Lord on a number of occasions emphasised that if we pray, believing that a prayer will be granted, it will be. Regarding these two miracles with the sun, I would have accepted that these things happened, but without marvelling, without really taking much notice of things that happened over three thousand years ago. Now, to have them confirmed by the US Space Agency, that really is impressive!

Much more recently than in the days of Isaiah God has performed another miracle with the sun. This took place on 13th October 1917 at Fatima, Portugal and was the sixth of the miraculous appearances at Fatima of the Blessed Virgin Mary to three child shepherds, Lucia, Francisco and Jacinta. Around one million people still make the pilgrimage to Fatima on 13th May, the date of the first appearance. Sue and I have visited at a less crowded period and it is a very special place, deeply revered by Roman Catholics and officially recognised by the Vatican. On 13th October 1917, some seventy thousand people were present, including nobility, clergy and journalists. The Virgin Mary had promised to perform a miracle on that day 'so that all may believe'. On her appearance that day, looking very sad, the Blessed Virgin said to the three visionaries: 'Do not offend the Lord our God any more, because He is already so much offended.' It had been pouring with rain all morning and everyone was soaked. At noon Lucia suddenly cried out: 'Look at the sun!' The multitude then saw what was afterwards called the 'Miracle of the Sun'. The following is the testimony of the reporter for the anti-clerical daily *O Seculo*: 'The sun looked like a plaque of dull silver. It neither burned nor blinded the eyes. It might have been an eclipse taking place, but at that moment a great shout went up and one could hear the spectators shouting: "A miracle! A miracle! A marvel! A marvel!" ' The crowd stood bareheaded and pallid with fear, eagerly searching the sky, the sun trembled, made sudden incredible movements outside all cosmic laws – the sun 'danced', according to the typical expression of the people. Jacinta's father stated: 'All eyes were fixed on the sky when the sun seemed to stop, and then began to move and dance. It stood still, then began to dance once more, until it seemed that it was being detached from the sky and was falling upon us. It was a terrible moment!' Many cried out: 'O Jesus! We are all going to die!' Others pleaded: 'Our Lady, help us!' There were some people who confessed their sins out loud. Finally, the sun stood still in its usual place. One last inexplicable marvel – all those people who had been drenched by the rain were suddenly completely dry!

In May 2000, after completing this book, there has been a further significant development. A revelation by the Virgin mary to the Visionaries in 1917 had been kept secret in a sealed envelope and the secret contents can now be revealed. The Visionaries had been made aware of 'a Bishop clothed in white who falls to the ground, apparently dead, under a burst of gunfire'. This describes the attempted murder of the Pope which took place in 1981 on May 13th, the date of the final appearance in 1917 of the Virgin Mary at Fatima and the miracle of the sun. On his first visit to Fatima, the Pope himself remarked: 'In the designs of Providence there are no mere coincidences.'

So, we have proof that God made the sun stand still to save Joshua's army, to go backwards to convince King Hezekiah and, less than a hundred years ago, to dance 'so that all may believe'.

There are several recorded appearances of the Virgin

Mary through the centuries in various parts of the world, including that to Bernadette at Lourdes, in France, in 1858. Lourdes is well known for the healing miracles which have occurred there and it is still visited each year by some two million pilgrims, many in search of healing. Visionaries have to face very long and intensive interrogation to ensure that appearances are genuine. Several, including Bernadette of Lourdes and Lucia of Fatima, have been made saints.

Of course, no human being understands all the sacred mysteries and ways of God, but those who spend their lives in prayer and service to God understandably have greater insight than we ordinary mortals in our materialist world. We have considered the contribution to faith of the saints and martyrs. In our own times also there are those who have been prepared to be tortured to death rather than deny their faith or betray their colleagues.

Miracles are certainly not confined to our Lord's time on earth, but are happening daily all over the world and it is the same with prayers being answered, then and now. The power of God's Holy Spirit, which was evident in the ministry of Paul and the disciples (see Chapter 8), is very much in evidence in our own times, as anyone truly desiring this awareness can discover. There is consistency in Christianity through some two thousand years, all true Christians being close to God and linked through Him, the source of life and power. That is the way it has always been and will be to the end of time.

If you have not yet found awareness of your spark of God and if you truly want to find Him, do continue to pray and God will answer. He needs you to come to Him and each one of us on earth has their own individual part to play.

Another reason why some people do not find God is that they believe themselves to be too evil to be accepted. Jesus understands this and is at pains to emphasise that this is never the case. The benefits of being a true Christian are endless: sense of purpose, real peace of mind, a new dimension of love, greater freedom from fear and worry, an ever-present source of strength and healing, discernment on courses of action and an open ear to prayer for any needs. Beyond all this God gives us a deeper dimension and meaning to our lives. Not too good to be true, just very, very good. And the cost? Being open to God, loving Him. If you do love Him you will show it by living as He wants us all to live, unselfishly, as clearly set down in the commandments and in Christ's teaching.

Of course there are eternal mysteries, things that we cannot understand. As St Paul states in 1 Corinthians 13:12: 'At present we see only puzzling reflections in a mirror, but one day we shall see face to face. My knowledge now is partial; then it will be whole, like God's knowledge of me.' If God always gave us just what we prayed for, and not what He considers best, then He would be Aladdin, not God.

Becoming a committed Christian is a transforming experience. One example is Mikie Heaton-Ellis, a bold young horseman, paralysed in a very bad fall and confined to a wheelchair. He then set himself up as a racehorse trainer. Mikie had been confirmed at school, believed in God and occasionally went to church but was not a committed Christian. He did not have a personal relationship with God. For some time after the accident Mikie relied on his own strengths, but eventually he realised that he could not fill the great hole in his life through his own burning ambition and striving. He eventually found what he was looking for in Jesus. Before the accident he had been at the centre of a rich, colourful world of horses, money and beautiful women and he was ruthless in getting what he wanted when he wanted. He had been angry with God since the accident but suddenly realised that God was angry with him. A vicar friend explained the steps he should take – to admit that he was a sinner and that he needed God; to believe that Jesus had died on the cross so that he could be forgiven; and to have the will to follow Jesus. He prayed that Jesus would take over his life. He continued this prayer for a few days. He read the Bible and he prayed; he began to talk about his faith and had a great sense of peace. He realised that God was truly with him and that he could cope with anything: 'What makes me tick is being a Christian – not just on Sundays, but twenty-four hours a day.' A few years later Mikie was diagnosed as suffering from motor neurone disease with a life expectancy of two years. He realised that the medical profession could not cure him. Instead of blaming God he said: 'I focus my attention on God. That helps me to have strength and to do what I want to do.' He also stated during this period that he had never been happier. In his biography it is recorded that he believed that the only dead certainty in this life is God's promise of eternal life.

We are all called to a personal loving relationship with Almighty God and it is a love that is capable of deepening to a dimension way beyond the bounds of human love. At the ultimate, there are saints who are reputed to have achieved true union with God. We have all got quite a way to go for that, but the important thing is to set out on the road. May you be richly blessed on the journey and may your spark be truly ignited.

Chapter 2

WHAT A LOVELY CHURCH THAT IS!

My wife and I were at a wedding reception in London and the lady addressing me was a fellow guest and a complete stranger. She had mentioned that she lived in London and her remark: 'What a lovely church that is!' referred to the church at which the wedding had just taken place. I followed up by asking which her church was. After a short pause she said, a little hesitantly: 'We don't go to church. We are not church people.' In these days, of course, this was a predictable response. My socially correct answer would have been: 'Of course not. I was wondering about the architecture of your local church.'

The lady wasn't backing off, so I continued: 'I have myself experienced the reality of God.' Then, very briefly, I told of my deep experience while walking on the evening of 24th June 1958, vibrantly aware of God's love pouring into me. I stopped and as I stood to pray I immediately became aware of God's presence beside me. I had heard discussions on what one would do if suddenly God appeared. Now I knew. He did appear. I sank to my knees in awe and immediately my head was flooded with the gold and silver light of God's glory.

An unexpected monologue from an unknown fellow wedding guest! By now my wife had come to the end of her conversation with the lady's husband and, noting that I was preoccupied, had moved on. Without waiting for any response I made my retreat, first planting an instinctive peck on the lady's cheek, no doubt considered as further proof of my nuttiness. Yet the encounter could bear fruit and I pray that it will.

In Christian terms, my most significant church meeting with a stranger was not at a wedding but at a funeral. John Dixey had been a close and loyal friend since pre-war days; we first met at Cambridge and then found ourselves on the same troop ship bound for India. John had told me about his close friend John Dee, who had recently become completely paralysed by a stroke. His wife, Elizabeth, had immediately dedicated her life to looking after John, doing absolutely everything for him. Sadly, not long after telling me about the Dees, John Dixey died. Sue, my wife, was unable to come with me to the funeral and, processing through the village from church to cemetery, I found myself walking beside a youngish, rather shy lady. As we walked we soon discovered that we had heard of one another through John Dixey. She was Elizabeth Dee. I arranged to visit Elizabeth and her husband in their little flat in a Sussex town. On my arrival John showed no sign of recognition, yet I felt at ease and found myself talking to Elizabeth about the Lord. She responded that she had been brought up as a Roman Catholic, but had opted out when she was seventeen. I told of my own deep faith and related to her my experience of God. I said that I felt certain that this experience had been given to be shared with others. Before leaving I gave her a copy of Bishop Morris Maddocks' *A Healing House of Prayer.*

Two or three weeks after my visit I had a letter from Elizabeth. Her mother had died, but in her last minutes Elizabeth had been able to say: 'I'm going to church again.' A faint smile had come to her mother's lips: 'I'm so pleased' she whispered and died in great peace. Elizabeth's husband, John, died peacefully in hospital in 1991 and we have faith that our prayers have been answered, that John is at peace in God's glory. Elizabeth now attends Mass daily at her church, where she became a founder member of a Healing Prayer Group and was instrumental in introducing healing services. She was elected to the parochial church council and deanery synod and became churchwarden at a critical period for the church. Elizabeth lives alone, leading an almost monastic life of simplicity and prayer and she has a Roman Catholic nun as her spiritual director. She is involved in much compassionate work, in addition to full-time employment in the Social Services, assisting disabled people. Consecrating her life to God, Elizabeth progressed further in faith and works in five years than I had in fifty. In 2000 she has been accepted back into the Roman Catholic Church and invited to try out her vocation as a nun in a Sussex Community.

I am one of those who truly believe in God the Three In One. More than this, I have experienced the reality of the personal love of God. This is a transforming experience and awesome – to be accepted with deep humility. Over the years I became aware that the experience was not given for my benefit alone but to be shared, so that others might seek it and more people be led to faith.

I calculate that in my lifetime I have attended at least four thousand services, in cathedrals, churches, chapels, monasteries, convents, halls, homes, hospitals, stadiums, arenas and parade grounds – mostly in England but in many overseas countries also. Most of these services were Church of England but others were Baptist, Roman Catholic, Methodist, Congregational, evangelical or occasionally Church of Wales, Church of Scotland, Christian Science or in a synagogue. It is relevant to state that before the Second World War going to church was the socially accepted thing to do, which undoubtedly helped attendance figures.

One is spoilt for choice when it comes to ways of worshipping Almighty God. One can be instantly aware of His presence in a tiny shepherd's hut, re-erected as a prayer chapel at Burrswood Christian Home of Healing in West

Sussex; in great cathedrals with the pomp and splendour of a ceremonial service, with thundering organ and glorious choir, processing office holders, bishops and priests; in an ancient, lovingly constructed parish church or in an ordinary room in a home with a gathering of worshipping Christians. God is everywhere for those who truly seek Him. God is spirit and those who worship Him must worship in spirit and in truth (John 4:24).

You can be a good and caring human being without being a Christian. You cannot be a good Christian without being a good and caring human being and going to church. You can go to church without being either a Christian or a good human being. Those who love God feel the need to join others in worship. One could liken this to attending a party in honour of a friend at which we also meet his other friends. God is always with us and if we love Him we feel the need to do what He wishes. Those wishes are clearly set out for us in the Scriptures. Above all, He wants us to be aware of His love for us and for us to respond by loving Him and doing His will. If we really do want to find God's love and to deepen our faith, it will happen. I can testify that it has happened to me, as to countless others.

'You are lucky you have faith. I go to church because it is good for the children and I enjoy the singing.' My friend, a brewery director, and I were on our way back from a Christian Business Discussion Group evening in 1957. I was surprised at his comment, for it had never occurred to me that people would be churchgoers if they did not believe. Many years later we met again at a Christian gathering. My friend had become a man of deep faith – and by then so had I.

In our country church congregation at Compton, before 1939, there was much greater emphasis on the importance of the correct Anglican form of service and on avoiding any similarity to Rome, than on such matters as evangelism. In those days my faith was not vibrant or Spirit-filled. I did not feel the need to discuss it with others: that was 'not done' and anyway one felt it somehow inappropriate to chat about faith. Those were my feelings even at the age of eighteen. After the War my outlook changed rapidly on the ecumenical front. On business visits abroad, particularly to the USA, I visited churches for a short time of prayer and in Roman Catholic churches I felt a more prayerful atmosphere than with other denominations; there were usually people praying there at any hour of the day. I continue to maintain contact with Catholic monks and nuns as well as with lay Catholic friends.

My father had been a churchwarden at St Nicholas, Compton for many years and it was a privilege for me to be elected to that office just after the War, at the age of twenty-six. A few months earlier, on the death of my mother, I had also become patron of the living of that church. My great great uncle George had been rector of the church for forty-nine years. I held the office of churchwarden for over twenty years; I did not find it a challenging or fulfilling task, nor was it in any way spiritual, but the job had to be done and my business life gave me all the challenge I needed. Strangely, it was through my business life that I came to God at a deeper level, as explained in Chapter 3.

I believe that I was able to do more for the church as patron than as churchwarden, by choosing the most suitable rectors, with the help of the bishop and of my wife Sue. Being a relatively small parish, Compton was particularly appropriate for a minister of more mature years and ours were all around their mid-fifties or older when they came. We were fortunate, for all of them were, in their own individual ways, sensitive, kind and caring, with deep reverence and love for God.

The Reverend Aelfric Hudson was at a parish near Farnham. In order to see him in action, Sue and I decided to attend Evensong, which we were told took place in a chapel.

We had some difficulty finding it and when we arrived the service had just started. We were concerned to note that the minister was not wearing a clerical collar – that would not do at Compton! A hymn was announced and it was with relief that we noticed the hymn-book was the *Congregational Hymnal*: obviously we had come to the wrong chapel and this was not the Reverend Hudson! The next Sunday we got it right. Aelfric Hudson greeted each member of the congregation after the service, as we all came out into the evening sunlight. 'Don't think I have seen you before. Are you down for a day?' 'Yes' we truthfully responded. Soon afterwards we invited Aelfric to come and visit us at Loseley. His opening words were: 'I remember you, you were just down for a day!' He was a big man, very lame from a First World War wound, but full of fun; he loved God and he loved people and cared about them. Not all clergy have this important gift. It was Aelfric Hudson, by then a canon, who was to become the first Honorary Chaplain of my company, Guildway.

At Epsom we went to hear Canon Guy Howard, a most conscientious and scholarly man, less rumbustious than Aelfric but equally caring and very sensitive. Guy was followed by Dick Hambly, an Army chaplain then at the Royal Chelsea Hospital, home of the Chelsea Pensioners. Sue and I were privileged to attend a service there which he was conducting. Dick was different from his two predecessors but equally dedicated to God and to the needs of the parish – kind, sensitive, humble and very caring. We were truly blessed by all three rectors and we are so grateful.

People came from miles around to worship at St Nicholas, Compton, yet few of those living in the council houses of the village were members of the congregation. Those who did attend usually came to Evensong. There have been Ferraris, Bristols, Jensens and Aston Martins in the car park and one bishop referred to it as 'The Compton Motor

Show'. It was not the fault of the rectors, but this is not what a parish church should be about. However, we were attracting people who did not find what they sought in their own parishes and who appreciated the sermons and the spirituality as well as the beauty of our church. We also had visitors from all corners of the earth, most of them aware of the simple beauty, as well as the sense of peace, stemming from a thousand years of prayer, worship and glorifying God. All through the war, I had with me a photograph of the Sanctuary of St Nicholas, Compton, because it meant so much to me, not for protection, though protection I certainly received to the point of frustration, but that is another story..

There were, and still are, many churches in London, especially in the East End and in other areas of poverty, need and unemployment, which have done a great deal to help the poor, the homeless and outcasts. The Crypt of St Martins-in-the-Fields, off Trafalgar Square, was well known as a refuge for the homeless. In my day there was certainly no desperate poverty in our parish but I suspect that our Lord would not have been impressed and we might have merited one of His more scathing comments. As a churchwarden, I accept my share of responsibility, but things at Compton were about to change.

The powers-that-be decided that Compton could not continue the centuries-old privilege of having its own full-time rector. We were to be merged to form the Hog's Back ministry, comprising the parishes of Compton, Shackleford, Peperharow, Puttenham, Wanborough, Seale and Sands. There was outrage in all these parishes and threats of rebellion. Compton appealed and the two churchwardens and myself as patron had a meeting with the bishop, at which we explained the importance of our church – almost one thousand years old, a gem that people all over the world came to see. This required a rector who could show visitors round and enthuse them in the faith. Visitors were told: 'For one thousand years, every day people have walked up the path to this church to pray . . . Here is the mark of the crusader and the cross he inscribed to mark the vow he made that on his return he would make a gift to the church. He did return.' It all fell on deaf ears, the decision had been taken and we must be obedient. The Hog's Back ministry proved unsatisfactory and a new and better arrangement was made after a year, linking Compton with Shackleford and Peperharow only.

The Reverend Nigel Nicholson, unlike the previous rectors, was a bachelor in his early thirties. We were Nigel's first parish as rector and he was full of energy, drive and ideas. Study Groups, Prayer Groups, Men's Groups, and Mum and Toddler Groups were formed and I had the privilege of working with Nigel in building up the healing ministry. I was appointed as one of three lay pastoral assistants, an office I hold at the time of writing, fifteen years later. Monthly healing services were held. They were arranged by the Godalming Guild of Health, of which I was a member. Led by the rector, before the service, we had an hour-long preparation at the rectory, with prayer. These services were well attended and people did receive benefit, although no dramatic physical healings were recorded.

Nigel and I had a number of pub lunches and walks at which we discussed ideas. We really were becoming a lively group of parishes and there was plenty of enthusiasm, especially among the young. The spiritual life of the parish was really being nurtured and we had quiet days and retreats as well as Bible Study and Discussion Groups. At times older members found the pace a bit hectic, being exhorted to attend, on different Sundays, all three churches in the group of parishes and to sample all the different services, as well as support some of the group meetings.

My duties as lay pastoral assistant were mainly in the field of the healing ministry, assisting the rector in visiting the sick and with healing services including, when required, laying hands on the sick. I also wrote a number of articles on healing for the Parish Magazine. There was still a great deal of ignorance among church people about the Christian healing ministry. Of course, we all knew about our Lord's healing miracles and that these were continued by Paul and the Apostles after the ascension, but before the 1960s it was assumed that the healing ministry long ago ceased to exist. It was a challenging and exciting commission to assist in bringing this important ministry into our group of parishes.

Things were going well, then sadly a deep division arose over the rector's proposal for a church room. Nigel felt very strongly that there was an urgent need for a room adjoining the church in which meetings and Sunday School could be held. Certainly this would be a great asset, particularly for the Sunday School, and there was the important bonus of a WC, the Village Hall being some two hundred yards from the church. We were a relatively wealthy parish and it ought not to be too difficult to raise the sum required for the building, but a much bigger problem arose which split the parish.

Although the Parochial Church Council had voted in favour of the new building, with only two against, there was strong opposition by the majority of those living in the parish, many of whom were not church members. They felt passionately that to erect a new building adjoining our gem of a Saxon/Norman church was sacrilege. They had a point and from the start Sue had courageously opposed the scheme. Nigel would not budge and felt that anyone opposing him was an enemy of the church. I had shared Nigel's thoughts on the need for his planned facilities, but I became even more concerned at the split in the parish and the very unchristian bitterness and resentment on both sides. I felt that, given time, another solution would emerge – and it did. After Nigel had moved on to a larger parish, the WC was installed in a small vacant brick-built shed on the church path and the Sunday School was offered a room in the adjoining Eastbury Manor, a retirement nursing home behind the church. As an added bonus, many bored, elderly residents enjoyed seeing the children and the parish was spared both the capital and running cost of a new building.

Most of us had been able to forgive and forget. This had been helped when in 1986 St Nicholas, Compton celebrated its millennium. Nigel excelled in organising the celebrations, managing to attract some great preachers including Archbishop Donald Coggan, Metropolitan Anthony Blum, and the Reverend Dr Martin Israel.

When Nigel was promoted to Cranleigh, one of the largest parishes in the diocese, I had been reinstated as joint patron with the bishop. My preferred candidate for rector was a New Zealander, then still in that country, who had advertised in the *Church Times*. Earlier he had worked in New Zealand with the Reverend Barry Kissell, well known in the Christian healing ministry, and for several years at St Andrews, Chorleywood with Bishop Pytches. Barry has travelled all over the British Isles and many countries abroad teaching on the healing ministry and particularly on the reality of the power of the Holy Spirit. My candidate also was charismatic and dynamic and our bishop, not very interested in the healing ministry, did not feel that my choice was appropriate for Compton, Shackleford and Peperharow. Maybe he was right, but we would have had a lively time!

The only suitable candidate to come forward for our group of parishes was the Reverend John Fellows from a parish in Chelmsford Diocese and originally a barrister. Sadly, for the first four years, John and his wife Lynne were both dogged by ill health. Their misfortunes started the day they arrived and they almost refused to move in.

Unfortunately, Sue and I had to be away and had written to apologise and explain, but the churchwardens had a difficult time. The building work was not complete, decorations were not as specified, floors were wet with varnish etc. It was a bad start. Soon afterwards their much-loved cat was killed on the road, a heavy piece of furniture fell and narrowly missed a visiting mother and her baby, there were family tragedies and bereavements and much more. This all put further strain on the churchwardens and we would all have understood if John had taken the view that somehow Compton was not the place to be, but to his great credit he persisted and gradually things got better.

A situation arose where John could have found himself in almost as difficult a situation as did Nigel over his church room. This concerned the proposal for a new organ at a cost of around £150,000. 'Only the best for God' they said but I was not certain that this was what God wanted and I was one of the two members of the PCC who abstained from voting. We are not a very musical church and we two members felt that, with so much world poverty and need, if we could raise a sum such as this we should send a very large donation to needy causes and make do with a cheaper organ. The word 'electronic' to our lady organist caused instant ignition! Fortunately, we had learned our lesson over the church room and I took the view, shared by my fellow abstainer, that we should be democratic and support the majority vote. I made the first donation. The organ is fine but the lady organist resigned not long after its installation. Tremendous efforts were made by the members of the Organ Committee to find the right organ, with visits as far afield as Ireland, and endless details were researched. Meanwhile, prodigious efforts were also being made by the fund-raising committee and its chairman to achieve the required £180,000.

I am still lay pastoral assistant with special responsibility for the healing ministry and convenor of a Healing Prayer

Group with six members, which meets twice monthly and prays for all members of the parishes known to be ill or in need, carrying out visits where appropriate. I have always felt that women tend to be better than men in compassionate work such as this and we are very fortunate in our three lady members. Our other male member is a very active evangelising Christian. We work harmoniously together and the close support of the rector is essential.

At the church, the laying on of hands is offered at the evening sung Eucharist once a month and we have occasional healing services, one memorable occasion being led by Bishop Morris Maddocks, founder, with his wife Anne, of Acorn Christian Healing Trust.

'I notice that when I pray coincidences happen, when I do not pray they do not happen.' These oft-quoted words of the late Archbishop William Temple are very meaningful; a number of examples are quoted in this book, the following being one.

On my return from a business visit to Saudi Arabia, I mentioned to a priest how good it was to be wakened at dawn by the call to prayer from the mosque, adding: 'What a pity that we do not have something similar in our religion.' 'But we do,' replied Father Brian, 'the Angelus, which we always ring in our church at 6 p.m.' Two or three weeks after this a retired Anglican priest applied for a cottage through a mutual friend, the Reverend Jocelyn Grundy. We happened to have a cottage available in the village and we also had a vacancy for a minister to take the services in our estate church of St Francis, Littleton. Coming back after visiting the church, Father John Clay said: 'Would you mind if I tolled the Angelus bell at 6 p.m. every evening?' John Clay, his wife Marjorie and their daughter, moved in a few weeks later and every evening at 6 p.m. John tolled the Angelus and often children came and helped with the ringing. Better than 'the voice from the mosque'!

Since 1945 we have held a monthly Eucharist at St Francis, Littleton. Before Compton parish was merged, the rector had officiated and when it joined the group of parishes, Littleton obviously had to be dropped so we had a vacancy. In those early years we often had just four or five in the congregation and the bishop advised: 'Close it down. Close it down.' Somehow I felt this was defeatist, feeling that a revival would come. Numbers gradually did pick up and in the early 1990s with the Reverend Pat Ashe we often had thirty or more. Sadly, we very seldom had any of the farm workers from the village and one wife was heard to say that they did not go, because the few that did, did so to please Jimmy (me). I do hope that I have not been the cause of keeping too many people from going to church.

Father John formed a Bible Study group and in 1977 we also started a monthly group, 'The Company of St Francis, Littleton', with the stated object of 'trying to become more meaningful Christians: to exercise compassion; to pray for those in need and where possible, to follow up prayer with action; to be a caring community and to throw out a bridge to those outside the church'. Of course, not everyone joined in but we certainly became much more active and caring.

At our meetings we had reports on anyone local whom we knew to be in hospital or needing help and we discussed what we could do for them and arranged visits, in addition to praying. People in hospital from the village, whether or not they were members of the church, found themselves being visited by church members. Extracts from my report on our first year illustrate what we were seeking to do:

We pray that we may develop and grow in accordance with God's will, so that we may serve Him more fully. There are still so many in the area that have real problems, people who could be helped . . . the sick in body, mind and spirit, the lonely, the bereaved, people with problems of many kinds . . . What more can we do to put religion in its true perspective for those with no faith – to relate God to everyday life and not to isolate Him in the Heavens for Sundays only. Faith is given to those who really seek it. Prayer is often answered through people.

Father Clay adds:

And all the community is built on and sustained by Our Lord's own presence in the Eucharist, which is offered on Tuesdays at 9.30 a.m. and Thursdays at 7 p.m., in addition to the monthly 10.15 a.m. service.

One wife, whose husband had left her, had her firewood chopped and other offers of help. A husband whose wife was in hospital had lunches brought to him and on one occasion two ladies, each bearing his lunch, collided at his gate! Sadly, in the space of a few years there had been a number of broken marriages and a suicide in our little hamlet. At least the Company of St Francis, Littleton was showing that the church did care and offered help. We had become a caring church, an active church. One person who had been brought up as an agnostic joined the group and it was a great day when he received confirmation in Guildford Cathedral. A further innovation was the December Carol Service, starting at the church and going down to sing carols with the cows at the adjoining farm, attracting many children.

Nothing goes on forever, but the end of the Company of St Francis, Littleton, which had seemed so practical and friendly, featuring Christian love in action, was sudden, sad and utterly unexpected. As often happens, human passions can take precedence over Christian virtues. Our meetings were friendly and informal, taking place in one another's homes and with no officially appointed chairman.

On this occasion I was unwittingly the culprit. On the farm we had been served with notice by the River Authority that we must forthwith cease to pollute the watercourses with effluent from our cows, or face prosecution. We hastened to install the prescribed slurry silo and the requisite pumping gear. This was a matter of great urgency; there was no alternative and I had not consulted the village residents. Unknown to us, the erection of the twelve-foot high slurry silo had angered several residents, who held meetings to consider what action could be taken but had not communicated with us. Sue and I first became aware that there was a problem when, at the monthly meeting of the Company of St Francis, Littleton, a passionate diatribe against us was delivered by one member and backed up by others. The atmosphere was electric. The hostess of the evening was in tears. I remember saying: 'What do you want? I have explained. I have apologised. I feel absolutely shattered. Perhaps, like St Francis, I should take all my clothes off and be left with nothing.'

It was so vindictive, so unexpected and obviously planned. The meeting dispersed. The next day, Sue received bouquets of flowers and there were messages of condolence; I called on the chief attack spokesman and we shook hands. Nevertheless, so unpleasant, so unchristian was that evening that for a long time none of us had the heart to continue. For the second time in my experience it had been forcibly demonstrated that Christian groups must apply Christian standards of humility, love and openness, and must be prepared to discuss prayerfully divisive issues. We had ignored our Lord's teaching: 'Anyone who nurses anger against his brother must be brought to justice' (Matthew 5:22). 'First go and make peace with your brother' (Matthew 5:24). Resentment and bitterness are truly evil and destructive. Reconciliation and openness are essential in all walks of life, especially in families and churches. When in doubt, pray. I have chronicled these two bitter experiences at Compton and Littleton in the hope that it may perhaps save another parish or group from suffering a similar fate.

In addition to being closely involved with both St Nicholas, Compton and St Francis, Littleton we also have a family burial chapel at St Nicholas, Guildford and officially we are in that parish. This is an Anglo-Catholic church and we have a cordial relationship with them and occasionally attend services there.

With so many churches it might seem strange that we have also instituted two chapels at Loseley in recent years. In September 1986 we converted a junk room at the top of the main staircase in the house. We cleared it out, laid a carpet in light blue, the healing colour, and put in a surplus pew from St Francis, Littleton. We needed a simple table for the altar; I had nothing in mind but in prayer it came to me that I should find a suitable table in an alcove in a disused upper area. I found it: a simple little oak table covered with a protecting sheet of hardboard. I was not conscious of ever having seen it before, but it was ideal. From the moment the chapel was furnished it had a wonderful sense of peace and people have found healing there. The chapel was dedicated on 9th September 1986 by Bishop Morris Maddocks. The bishop presided at the Eucharist, assisted by our chaplain, the Reverend Pat Ashe, who devised the special service. The only embellishment was the engraving of the dove of the Holy Spirit in the top of the window. The window is of clear glass, giving a view of the creation below, the woods and fields, often with grazing cattle and sheep. If anyone had told me when we dedicated the chapel that we would be building a new one within ten years I would not have believed it – but we did.

Any city possessing a cathedral is enriched by it. If time permits, even for the non-committed Christian, a visit to the local cathedral can be an experience not be missed. I have recorded in *The Loseley Challenge* the deep experience of visiting St Peter's in Rome. Guildford, Coventry and Liverpool are the only dioceses to have a cathedral built after the Second World War. I have had connections with Guildford Cathedral from the early days of construction and was privileged to be present at its consecration by the Archbishop of Canterbury in the presence of Her Majesty the Queen in 1961. The cathedral is situated just outside the town at the top of Stag Hill, with Surrey University on the north slope of the hill and the Royal Surrey County Hospital at the foot. All built since the War, there is now provision for body, mind and spirit, all sharing the hill, with the spirit appropriately at the top.

The creation of something to the glory of God brings tremendous satisfaction. I had not realised how very rewarding this was until we created our two little chapels. Just think what those who created the great works of our Christian heritage must have felt – the architects, designers, stonemasons and other craftsmen, the artists who created the stained glass windows, the great composers and the writers of hymns, the composers of church music and the organ builders. For the scriptures we have to thank the inspired authors of all the books in the Old and New Testaments and the scholars who produced the translations in many different editions. Beyond imagination is the amount of dedicated toil that has been expended in producing all these masterpieces down the ages, produced to give glory to God. Thousands upon thousands of people gave their lives in toil in their own particular spheres and according to their individual gifts. Some even suffered death for their efforts, including Archbishop Cranmer, among whose contributions to our liturgy was the 1662 prayer book, still in use. His Church rewarded him by burning him at the stake.

We are the beneficiaries, profiting from the works of those who have gone before and having responsibility for putting whatever gifts we may have to add, in our generation, to use for God's glory. There are indeed, in every church, splendid people doing just that, employing their particular gifts and talents, perhaps not as architects or artists, but as flower arrangers, singers in the choir, administrators, fund raisers, needlewomen, surveyors, builders, drivers etc. We all have different gifts and the greatest gift for the church is people who care.

Friendly people are needed who will welcome newcomers. I have known people who have been discouraged from attending a church because no one welcomed them or showed any friendship or encouragement. One of these was a lonely man who had recently lost his wife; he was badly in need of warmth and friendship. There is an opportunity for prayerful people to join or lead a prayer group, praying for the sick and for the needs of the parish. People trained in the ministry of healing are needed to visit the sick in hospital or at home, to lay on hands when requested and to assist at healing services. Visiting people who are ill does need to be done sensitively and quietly, particularly in a hospital ward, where the visitor either prays silently or in a whisper, so that only the patient can hear. Some people are burning to evangelise and there is always work to be done in outreach – encouraging others to come and join the church. Others may say: 'I could not do any of these.' Have you tried?

In my young days, lessons at services were read by churchwardens and dignitaries, but there are many who can read really well and they are now more likely to be given the opportunity, if they offer. Lifts to church and help with shopping for those without transport, especially the elderly and infirm, are greatly appreciated and many churches organise these functions through volunteers.

On the day that I was finalising this chapter there was an article in the *Daily Telegraph* by Mary Killen, headed: 'We love to go to church but only when it's empty.' The article reported that only 7.5 per cent of the population of England worshipped regularly and that the biggest fall was in 'trendy' churches, the traditionals holding their own in the past year. It was also indicated that an increasing number of people were visiting churches when there was no service on. Eighty-four-year-old Mrs Betty Parsons stated: 'I could not live a day of my life without my faith and I still go to church, but only when there's not a service.' Many people take this view, preferring an empty church in which to find peace and quiet – and hopefully the presence of God. One certainly agrees with the need for peace and stillness in our busy world, but we do need to think of what God wants, not just what we want. God needs to be worshipped and glorified and this can be done better by a congregation led by a minister, and perhaps with organ and choir, rather than by sitting on our own at peace. We can do this without being in church. People who only visit a church that is empty cannot be part of the church community.

Whether churches and cathedrals are visited when empty or full, the wonderful thing is that they exist. Thank God for them, for those who have constructed and adorned them and those who maintain them and worship in them.

In addition to the praise and worship and adoration of God, the church plays a vital part in the Christian life – not only through worship and prayer but in teaching, hearing the Scriptures and in caring for those in need. Our Lord always glorified the Father but He also emphasised the importance of serving not only God but our fellow beings on earth. This was forcibly demonstrated by the parable of the sheep and the goats: 'Anything you did for one of my brothers here, however insignificant, you did for me' (Matthew 25:31–46).

We serve God in our daily lives and we come together in church to worship Him. Church plays – or should play – an important part in the development of our faith, but faith also develops in the course of our daily lives. Some of the milestones in my own faith journey are charted in the next chapter and beyond.

Chapter 3

MILESTONES ON A CHRISTIAN JOURNEY

One needs to be sensitive in the matter of sharing personal Christian faith. To those who do not believe, the believer may appear to be stupid, gullible, presumptuous etc. Jesus faced far worse accusations: blasphemy, subversion, sedition, and being a friend of prostitutes and sinners.

Humility is essential. More important than what we say is to live our faith and try to follow our Lord's teaching and example. In my case, faith has grown during my passage through life. Each human being is different and years ago I made a note of a remark that I overheard: 'Like drink or the Church or anything else, if they want to go after it, it's up to them!' That's one way of putting it and it is a fact that it is up to each individual. We have complete freedom of choice whether to follow Christ or reject Him. That is the way it has been for two thousand years.

There are so many false impressions about God, the Church and the Christian life. There are also many idols – money and possessions, pleasures, passions and technology – which tempt people away from the worship of Almighty God. These idols hold hearts and minds arguably more firmly than would any 'graven image'. The good news is that it is never too late to come to Christ.

I suppose most of us start off by thinking that Christianity means going to church, which is about as accurate as saying that being an MP means going to the

House of Commons. In both cases it is not only what you do when you get there that counts but what you do in your daily life. It is in our daily lives that we serve God and many people who do not regard themselves as Christians are indeed living in accordance with God's will. They help others, show respect for authority, support the weak, and help those in trouble. If only these people were prepared to acknowledge the existence of God their lives would be enhanced and transformed. They would gain much and lose nothing of true worth.

It could be said that the spiritual journey starts at birth, for parents and home life do have an influence, though less so now than in the days of my childhood. People can find God at any stage of their lives and many of the most dedicated Christians have been late-comers. The spiritual journey is the most important journey that anyone can make.

My own home background, between the wars, was founded on duty – duty to God, to the King, to the British Empire etc. It sounds depressingly dull, but it was a helpful beginning, for I believed and took God seriously. However, it was not until I had reached the age of thirty-eight, on that evening in Wales, that I discovered the reality of the love of God and this was perhaps the greatest milestone in my journey. Nothing has been quite the same since then. There are, of course, many reasons why people do not find faith in God. There is much misunderstanding about Christianity and, in many cases, a complete lack of spiritual awareness, but each one of us does have a spiritual dimension and each one is born with a spark of God. My hope is that in outlining my own spiritual journey, I may be able to help a few fellow travellers on their way. Our Lord exalted the humble and meek. Humility and love are the main ingredients.

In my childhood the Ten Commandments were taken

very seriously and church members were expected to set an example. I accepted the duty of going to church every Sunday, but admit to finding it usually more boring than uplifting, particularly at school with services daily in chapel, twice on Sundays and three times if one went to Communion. Fortunately my faith was sufficient to prevent my dropping out.

Vital to our progress on the Christian journey are the people we meet. Some are encouragers, some set an example to follow. I am deeply grateful to the many who have helped me on my spiritual journey, including the monks and nuns, one archbishop, a number of bishops, priests and deacons and very many other people of all denominations and, of course, my parents. Two people must receive special mention for their help on my Christian journey. The earliest is Lucy Coltham, a simple and wonderful spinster, some thirty-years older than me, who in my earliest years lovingly and patiently shared with me her simple and unshakeable faith in God through Christ Jesus. I owe her far more than I ever repaid and I continue to give thanks to God for her.

Next was David Hurford. David and I first met on the evening of 18th July 1940 when we joined the Army as troopers at the Royal Tank Regiment Training Depot at Farnborough. There were about thirty of us, mechanics, stable lads, tailors, gardeners, all sorts. David, large, cheerful and a successful rugby player and cricketer was someone I would normally have been shy of, but we got on well from the moment we met. David, at a younger age than would now be accepted, was a Franciscan Tertiary, the Third Order founded by St Francis for lay people who continued in their normal occupations and lived at home, but kept strict rules on prayer, work and lifestyle. We had adjoining beds in the barrack room and I followed his example in kneeling to pray before getting into bed. I would never have considered doing this on my own, but I believe that we were respected by many in the barrack room. There was certainly no ridicule, to the great credit of our fellow troopers. After two months, we passed out as Officer Cadets to Sandhurst where David and I shared a room and eventually we were commissioned into the same regiment. At that stage of life, being close to someone who was an active and dedicated Christian and with whom one could openly discuss matters of the faith was a tremendous bonus. A very important milestone. After the War we became godparents to each other's sons. David was lively and full of fun and often said he did not want to grow old and dependent. His wish was granted, but far too soon, for very sadly, he died of a heart attack in his fifties.

I wanted to write of another significant wartime Christian friendship but then so many more names came into my mind, people who have helped and supported me along the road – not only with spiritual guidance and encouragement but with kindness and support and help in various ways. We cannot journey by faith alone and Christians cannot claim a monopoly on kindness, caring and love. Lucy and David were so special at crucial times in my life. In this chapter they represent the many people along the road – helpers, encouragers, colleagues, friends – to whom my warm gratitude extends. Thank you all. May you be richly blessed.

As well as being influenced by individuals, my spiritual life has developed through a number of channels and experiences. The Provost of Guildford's Industry Discussion Group in 1957 was a significant milestone. One evening we were addressed by Sir Alfred Owen, a dedicated Christian and chairman of Rubery Owen, at that time the largest private company in the UK. In the course of his talk, Sir Alfred told us how he gave his Christian testimony on the occasion of his twenty-first birthday. 'Nail your colours to the mast,' he urged. Encouraged by this, on 14th February 1958, I gave my own public testimony at the opening of the new offices of my company, Guildway Limited. Our rector, Canon Aelfric Hudson, was inducted on that day as Honorary Chaplain to the firm. From that day on we were aware that the firm had labelled itself 'Christian' and we had to be even more conscientious in our dealings and in the way in which we looked after our employees and all who dealt with us.

It was generally acknowledged that Guildway had a high quality reputation and everyone in the company was aware of this. I insisted on high standards of conduct and once dismissed an executive for lying to me – this was before the Industrial Relations Act! In the years ahead I learned a great deal about Christianity in business. In particular, I came to realise that I could best serve God in my business by being known as a Christian and, without making reference to religion, by striving to set an example and operate on Christian principles. Such principles should include truth, fairness, openness and consideration for individuals, whether employees or customers, suppliers, advisors or bankers. It was in compassion that I have felt led to serve and to minister in the name of Christ. When people are in trouble – as a result of sickness, bereavement or marriage breakdown – that is when they need help and that is the opportunity for giving them the most valuable help of all: awareness of Almighty God.

That 1958 Valentine's Day was a significant signpost on my journey. I had not realised before what an important step it was to proclaim my faith in public. I am now certain that it was this that led to the deep experience of God on 24th June the same year. Sue, our son Mike, then seven years old, and I were staying in a cottage in the Mawddach Estuary, Wales. After supper in the evening I usually went out on my own for a walk and to pray. Praying outside at night was something I had picked up in the War. The clear, star-spangled sky and the moonlight over the vast stillness of the desert had provided a wonderful setting for prayer. Certainly an improvement on the barrack room. There is a sense of awe, an awareness of the vastness of Creation. The Welsh evening of 24th June 1958 was particularly lovely, with a clear sky and soft sunlight.

I walked along the riverbank, then across the road to a footpath leading up the hill. As I approached the hill I felt a very strange sensation, of love pouring into my head. This continued for several seconds. I could not understand why this should be happening. I then suffered intense abdominal pain for a short spell and by then the flow of love had ceased. I walked on up the path, a young plantation of fir trees on the left and a low dry stone wall on the right, with a view across the river valley to the distant hills. I stopped to pray. Immediately I became aware of the presence of God. He was close to me on my right side. I did not look, for I knew that I would not see Him, though I was absolutely certain of His presence. At that moment I did not need to think, I just fell to my knees in front of the stone wall. I was then flooded with light, glorious bright, gold and silver light all through my head. I was aware that I was experiencing the glory of God. I do not know how long I stayed there, but eventually I got up and started to walk up the hill. I knew that God had made Himself known for a purpose. He must want me to do something for Him. I asked Him to let me know what He wanted, expecting an instant response. I walked slowly on up the hill, full of expectation. I stopped, alert . . . I walked on . . . I stopped. Sue would be getting worried and before it got dark I returned to the cottage.

God's timing is different to ours. It was not hours, but eighteen years that I had to wait for my next experience, which led to the Christian healing ministry and to the care of cancer patients. Increasingly, I have become aware that the testimony I gave on 14th February that year was related to this experience, a sort of trigger. If one gives something to

God He will return it a thousandfold. Eighteen years later an offering of love to God also proved to be a trigger.

We are often impatient but God knows best. Although a purpose was not made known to me that evening in Wales, I knew that one day it would be revealed and in the meantime I must improve. There was plenty of room in my life for improvement. It was to be a period of preparation and I knew that eventually God would make known His purpose for me – and He did. In my period of waiting I experienced a thirst for deeper spiritual knowledge and awareness. My search included the reading of books, such as *Nine O'Clock in the Morning*, which made me aware of the reality of the power of the Holy Spirit today. Reading this book was a milestone on my journey, although I do have reservations about it. For instance, I do not believe in praying for such personal benefits as parking spaces or fine weather! Nevertheless, like millions of others, I have discovered the ingredient that so many people miss, the reality of the power of the Holy Spirit, a subject that appears many times on my journey.

I went on retreats, attended Christian seminars and lectures, went to Christian gatherings, talked with monks and nuns, including Father Manson. Toby Manson was awarded the Military Cross serving under my father in the First World War, and in his later years spent his summer vacations with Sue and I at Loseley. In addition to his sanctity, he had twinkling eyes and a lovely sense of humour ('If you pour boiling water down a rabbit hole what do you get? Answer: Hot cross bun!').

Mary Margaret, Mother General of the Sisters of St Francis and Divine Motherhood, was another close friend of ours who was a great help to me at this time. The Mother House and farm of this Catholic order was nearby and I acted as advisor on farming and land use. Although Sister Mater Dei, who ran the farm, was alleged to have a ripe vocabulary, I never heard anything unseemly from her sweet lips, not even when, on my advice, farming operations were terminated. In fact, Mater Dei and I continued our harmonious relationship. I was privileged to attend services in the nuns' chapel at Ladywell Convent, as the only male and the only Anglican in the congregation. I was always made welcome, although sadly Anglicans are forbidden to receive the sacrament at a Catholic Mass.

In November 1958, on a business visit to the USA, I was delighted to find myself staying in the same motel in Indianapolis as Billy Graham. He was speaking at the Indianapolis Stadium on the evening Fred Gooch and I arrived. I was one of the last to arrive at the packed stadium and had to go right to the top to get a seat. At the end of his talk Billy Graham assured us that we were all 'saved' but that anyone having any doubt regarding their own personal salvation should come forward. I certainly did not feel able to claim 'I am saved', so I got out of my seat for the long and embarrassing walk to the arena, aware of thousands of eyes upon me. The music became soft and the evangelist asked everyone to pray for those coming forward. 'However great their sins, God will forgive them. Pray . . . softly pray.' Very few had moved from their seats and I felt very self-conscious. Gradually, with encouragement from the evangelist, the numbers coming forward grew to a few hundred out of the ten thousand or more in the stadium. For each of us there was a pair of counsellors waiting, who showed us to seats and sat down on either side. I explained that I was not aware of any particular sin; I was a churchwarden, I ran a company that made houses and I was a farmer producing food and we shared our profits. I had received much but I realised that there were sins of omission and that I had many faults. The counsellors were unable to persuade me that I was 'saved' and in exasperation called in an ordained minister who was no more successful. I felt very strongly that salvation was

God's prerogative and that it was presumptuous to assume that one was saved. Scripture was quoted to me in assurance of my salvation but I felt extremely uneasy on the matter. Later that evening in my hotel I tried to telephone Billy Graham in his room but, understandably, no calls could be put through.

The following Sunday I attended a service at Washington Roman Catholic Cathedral. By coincidence the preacher used the same text as Billy Graham, the parable of the sower. I managed to meet him after the service and explained my concern. To my great relief, the priest fully understood my predicament and agreed that salvation was certainly God's prerogative.

I am an admirer and firm supporter of the inspired work and teaching of Dr Graham, who may well have brought more people to the Lord in his lifetime than anyone else in the twentieth century. The fact that not all his converts remain in the churches is not Billy Graham's responsibility but that of the churches and of the converts themselves. As our Lord reminds us in the parable of the sower, there are many reasons for people falling away after receiving the word of God. These things do not change.

At the invitation of a business friend, Sue and I attended a number of Moral Re-Armament (MRA) meetings and dined at an imposing house in Berkeley Square. We were also invited to attend the excellent film on Africa, *Freedom*, at a lovely Sussex farmhouse and after a great deal of coaxing I agreed to accompany our business friend on a weekend at the MRA World Headquarters at Caux, Switzerland. There were some two thousand delegates attending, but at the 8 a.m. Sunday Anglican Eucharist, with an African bishop officiating, there were only a dozen people as this service coincided with an important conference session. We were impressed by the young people we met in MRA – clean, cheerful, non-smoking, non-drinking, non-promiscuous and the women did not use make-up. Yet, somehow, we never felt quite at ease. It was moral rather than spiritual. An eminent Christian friend commented that he could not get on with MRA people, but that those who had been members and had left the movement tended to be splendid! I have since read that Archbishop William Temple made a similar observation. Cuthbert Bardsley, later to become Bishop of Coventry, was very involved in the development of the movement in its earlier days but eventually left for the same fundamental reason: that not enough prominence was given to Christianity.

Our dalliance with MRA came to an abrupt end. Sue, Mike and I were invited to attend an MRA play at the Westminster Theatre, London. I was irritated, embarrassed and offended by the presumptuousness of the play – there was a red telephone on stage through which conversations with God were enacted. I must have been more disturbed by the play than I realised. The next day I completely lost my memory. I could not remember the name of someone who had been at Loseley all my life, nor could I remember the names of our fields. Fortunately, this lapse only lasted about three hours, but I had to inform our friend that I had received clear guidance that I must cease contact with MRA.

So many people fail to find faith because they have false ideas about the nature of religion. Our young friend Giles had just left school and was about to go off to India to find spirituality among the gurus of the East. He was incredulous when I told him that God was here now, that He still worked miracles, that people are healed through prayer, that the Holy Spirit is much in evidence these days, that I had witnessed men and women being released from evil spirits, that a number of times I had heard people speaking 'in tongues', a language quite unknown to them, and that occasionally at large gatherings somebody with the gift of interpreting tongues had given the translation of the words.

I also mentioned the 'fruits of the Spirit', including peace, love and joy, all of which can be experienced at a deeper spiritual level. Man is created with a spiritual nature and, without an awareness of God, we are missing out on our third dimension. When blessed with spiritual awareness our lives become so much more meaningful, especially with the realisation that we are in eternal life.

I was introduced to Roy Calvocoressi, who ran a Christian Centre at his London home. A deeply committed Christian with considerable flair, Roy founded CHIPS in the cause of world peace and travels extensively in the interests of developing world peace through the Christian message. Another of his enterprises was CIEL – Christian Industrial Enterprises Limited – which encouraged Christian-led businesses. Although excellent in theory, I was disturbed to hear one of the members publicly proclaiming that every time the firm's order book dried up he prayed and the orders flowed in! Not many years before that my own business had been threatened with liquidation. It had never occurred to me to pray for orders or for finance or even for the bank manager to be friendly. What I did pray for was for strength and discernment. These I received in full measure which in turn led to my testimony on 14th February 1958.

It was at one of Roy Calvocoressi's gatherings that I was introduced to FGBMFI – Full Gospel Businessmen's Fellowship International – a Christian organisation founded in the USA which now has thousands of chapters worldwide. The main function of the chapters is to arrange breakfasts or teetotal dinners in local hotels and I have attended some of these in London and Guildford. Christian members are encouraged to bring a non-believer as a guest. At the end of the meal there is singing of Christian hymns and songs, testimony from one or more members and usually a guest speaker. Prayer with laying on of hands is offered to anyone present wishing for healing and I have witnessed some remarkable healings at these meetings as well as hearing very powerful testimonies. Many orthodox Christians are uneasy about such informal evangelical initiatives, but our Lord healed not in the temple but wherever the sick person happened to be – in the street, by the pool, or in their bedroom. Certainly, the dignity and formal reverence of the normal church service are lacking, but initiatives such as FGBMFI are important, for they make people, including non-churchgoers, aware of the reality of the power of God. He is not dead, He is not even asleep: He is still performing miracles!

The foregoing are some of the signposts and milestones that have helped me on my way. Some of my milestones would have been seen by others and they, in turn, will have seen many that I have missed. There are countless signposts and milestones on the roads of life along which we travel. It is important that we watch and listen in expectancy. Each human being is different and we are not all called along the same road, but in accordance with our gifts and talents. The gifts are given for the benefit of God's Church, the cause of Christ.

Earlier I recorded how I was transformed by experiencing the reality of the powerful love of God. Until that moment I had been aware academically of God's love, which was quite different from experiencing the real thing. In November 1999, when I was aged seventy-nine, I had a similar experience with the peace of God. This has always been important to me and I chose 'The peace of God that passeth all understanding' as my prayer in the BBC *Prayer For Today* programme. The only text in our chapel is: 'My peace I leave with you', in the west window. Like the experience of God's love, the experience of His peace was unexpected and dramatic.

Both my parents had lost their memory when they were younger than I am now and I have had the occasional lapse.

This time it was sudden and horrifying: speaking to Sue, I suddenly could not think of the next word. I knew what I wanted to say but could not find the words. I was stammering, groping for words, helpless, whereas moments before I had been speaking quite normally. I was distraught. Suddenly, a most wonderful sense of peace descended on me – peace and love. I just knew that this was of God, for the peace was so deep and blissful. 'I don't care if I have lost my memory; I am happy, at peace, all is well.' That was the spiritual coming to my aid when the mental failed. Happily, normal memory and speech were immediately restored and at the time of writing continue to be maintained. More important, I no longer fear, for if I do lose my memory – or for that matter my life – I know that all will be well. The purity and depth of that peace was such that only God could provide. I had not prayed for it, I was not aware that such depth of peace existed, although I now remember that I had experienced it, many years ago and to a lesser degree, in a dream. God knew my need and in that instant I was healed. Thanks be to God. I suggest that it is worth spending a few moments reflecting on John 14:27, AV:

'Peace I leave with you, my peace I give unto you: not as the world giveth, give I unto you. Let not your heart be troubled, neither let it be afraid.'

Chapter 4

LEADING TO HEALING

I am surprised to see from my diary that it was not until July 1974 that I first became aware that there was a Christian healing ministry and that people in our times could be healed through prayer. I was attending a conference in Oxford and decided to go to a lunch hour service in one of the churches. Towards the end of the service, the Anglican minister explained that there was a Christian ministry of healing. Anyone wishing to go up and kneel before the sanctuary rail would receive prayer and laying on of hands for healing. I was not in need of healing but I was fascinated by the concept of divine healing and a number of people did go forward.

A few weeks later Sue and I attended a lecture on the Christian healing ministry in the refectory at Guildford Cathedral. We were very interested, but had no inkling of how significant this ministry was to become for us. Not long after this, I went on a retreat led by the Reverend Doctor Martin Israel, on the subject of Christian healing. Not only a leading pathologist, author and lecturer at the Royal College of Surgeons, Martin Israel was also an ordained Anglican minister and a revered mystic. On this retreat I expected to learn how to lay on hands and to be taught appropriate prayers for healing. None of this. 'The Christian ministry of healing is about being OPEN, open to God and to the needs of our fellow beings.' Martin spoke for two days without any notes, but I think that this was his only reference on how to conduct healing.

One day I asked Bridget, a young mother in our congregation, if she was aware of the Christian healing ministry. She replied that her brother-in-law, the Reverend David Payne, was engaged in this ministry as Warden of the Divine Healing Mission at Crowhurst in East Sussex. I soon found myself having a meal with David and Anne Payne at Crowhurst and received prayer and laying on of hands from them. I later attended two excellent one-week courses on the Christian healing ministry there, and was invited back to give talks to subsequent courses. On entering the chapel at Crowhurst one is permeated by a depth of peace and love, which is very special. It is a modern, simple, hexagonal building; the atmosphere of love, prayer and worship need no adornment. Many people have been transformed by a short stay. Crowhurst and other splendid places for Christian refreshment and healing are listed in Appendix 2.

It can be lonely as an active Christian in a world that regards spirituality as verging on lunacy. This is probably why at this period I joined in so many Christian activities. These included the Godalming Christian Lunch Club. One of their speakers was a former inmate of Broadmoor, who had a deep experience of God while in prison and gave his life to the Lord. He has written books and is a regular public speaker. There was also a variety of other local Christian business meetings. A senior civil servant and his wife hosted monthly Christian evening meetings in their lovely house near Guildford. The Rosminion Friars held charismatic evenings at Wonersh, which I sometimes attended. For me the most significant group became Bronwen Astor's charismatic prayer group at Tuesley. It was when I first attended one of these evenings that I received the power of the Holy Spirit, a completely unexpected and deep spiritual experience, which led me to minister to cancer patients.

Before the meeting, I had mentioned to Bronwen that I

had two friends seriously ill with cancer, who needed prayer. About ten of us sat round the room in a semi-circle. We listened to a recorded address by Cardinal Suenens. Then we sang a hymn. A short silence. Then a prayer, followed by a reading of scripture. Then another hymn . . . Then it happened. Bronwen, sitting opposite me, said: 'James has two people he wants us to pray for.' As she was speaking I felt, as it were, a swarm of bees coming from her forehead through mine. Not actual bees, of course, but the power of the Holy Spirit, perhaps in the form of electrical energy. It was over in a flash, but the effect has been permanent. From that instant I had enhanced compassion, I felt the call to visit the sick and the need to meditate and now I had the ability to do so. I also had a clear understanding of the nature of the Trinity. In that instant my life had been changed. There is no doubt that it was from God, for it took place at a Christian prayer meeting where God was praised in the singing of hymns and in prayer and His word was read aloud from the Bible.

It was some weeks before I realised that this experience was a call to minister to cancer patients. The first of these was to be Harry, a mechanic with my firm Guildway. Harry was unconscious in the intensive care unit of the hospital and dying. The next of kin had been informed that he had just hours to live and his functions were gradually failing. I prayed over him and two days later Harry was in a ward, sitting up in bed and drinking tea. He was in remission for a year, during which he came back to work part-time. When Harry died, all the family, the chaplain and I were present. Harry's parents said they found it much easier to come to terms with his death than if it had occurred a year earlier. I said: 'We must thank God.' They assured me that they did, although they were not church people and had not been aware that I had actually prayed over Harry. It is important to give glory to God for healings, but in this case the non-

Christian parents would have given me the credit, so I was reluctant to tell them that I had prayed over him. If there had been a nurse or someone who could have laid on hands with me, there would not have been a problem. A Christian remarked after Harry died: 'That was because the glory was not given to God.' I do not believe that was the cause, but I have read of a case where this did happen.

An Australian lady received complete healing of a very serious heart condition through prayer and laying on of hands. She was too embarrassed to mention that she had been healed by God, so gave credit to her doctor. She lost the healing and was aware of the reason. She later flew from Australia to America and received a second and permanent healing at a vast gathering under the ministry of the well-known Christian healing practitioner Catherine Khulman.

At this period I had not been trained as an official member of the Christian healing ministry; I was an enthusiastic 'one man band', full of faith and love of the Lord, full of compassion and feeling led to pray with the sick for healing. These were fulfilling and exciting days and some wonderful things happened, but I now realise that today anyone acting on his own, as I was, would have been regarded by the official Christian healing ministry as suspect. We are instructed, for good reasons, to work in pairs, although often this is not practicable. I did work prayerfully and sensitively. I felt led to people, never forced myself on anyone and always gave the glory to God. It so happens that my early patients were not church people. They received significant remissions and each of them came to a deeper awareness of God before they died.

During this time a mutual friend told me about Eve, a twenty-six-year-old hospital nurse who was very ill with cancer in Westminster Hospital. She was in much pain, very fearful, had no faith and was often in tears. Her husband, an Army corporal, could not accept the situation. I wrote to Eve that I was certain that she could be helped by God, although at that stage she might not be physically healed. I stated that I was not an ordained minister but I had a deep faith and would be happy to visit her in hospital, but would quite understand if she did not want that. Eve telephoned, inviting me to visit and on the next Sunday evening I went up to the Westminster Hospital.

Eve was a lovely girl, with deep brown eyes and black hair, which I was soon to discover was a wig; as is quite usual, she had lost her hair as a result of chemotherapy. We chatted and I talked of the Lord and His love. 'No use talking to me about eternal life; I'm not a Christian; I never go to church,' said Eve. I assured her that God loved her, mentioning that even the robber crucified with our Lord had received the assurance: 'This day you will be with me in Paradise.' I laid my hands on her head and, with Eve's permission, prayed slowly and softly.

I visited Eve weekly, going first to the lovely hospital chapel to pray and prepare. At 5 p.m. one afternoon, sitting at my desk, I had the overwhelming feeling that I should not wait until the usual 5.30 p.m. but go at once to the hospital. I arrived at about 6 p.m. to be met by Eve's husband and twin sister. 'So sorry James, you have made an abortive journey; no one is allowed to see Eve this evening. She is under anaesthetic and being examined to find the cause of serious internal bleeding; she is losing six pints of blood a day. We tried to telephone you to stop you coming, but you had left early. We are going home now; we thought at least we should wait until you came.' As they left, I knew that I was going to see Eve. I went to the chapel and prayed for her and for all those caring for her. I meditated, then sensed that the time had come to go to Eve's curtained cubicle in Marie Celeste Ward. One nurse was coming out and, as I entered, another was tucking up the blankets. Eve's husband and sister had been turned away, yet here was I, being allowed in without question. I knelt by the bedside and Eve, just coming round from the anaesthetic, whispered, barely audibly: 'I'm going to Jesus.' I softly replied: 'Not yet, Eve.'

I was overjoyed to hear those words from Eve, remembering that her words only a few months before had been: 'No good talking to me about eternal life'! That night the operation took place to locate the internal bleeding; there was no indication of the source until, instinctively, one of the surgeons put his finger on a spot and blood spurted. The cause identified, the bleeding was cured. Eve did get better and became strong enough to come down to our home with her husband for a weekend. Sadly, after a few months she relapsed again. Eve received the sacrament of anointing with holy oil from our friend Father James Naters SSJE and she died peacefully.

About three months later I returned to Westminster for a retreat led by the same Father James Naters. Walking past the Westminster Hospital, Eve was in my thoughts and the cancer patients now in hospital, fearful and in pain, without faith or awareness of God. Eve had been transformed through finding God. 'What can we do?' I asked myself, as I walked on to Westminster Cathedral to pray. On my return to the Retreat House, the first thing that Father Naters said was: 'There is someone that may be able to help, Berthe Hess, a Jewish artist who has painted a picture of 'The Living Christ'. She asserts that it was inspired by God to bring awareness of Christ's love and compassion to the sick, the suffering and the dying.' 'Amazing' I exclaimed, the one thing that has been on my mind all afternoon. Yet another case of 'when I pray coincidences happen!'

I went to meet Berthe Hess and her daughter Mauricette at their studio near St Paul's Cathedral and I at once sensed the sadness and compassion conveyed by the picture, particularly in the eyes. Berthe asked me to arrange for it to be unveiled in St Paul's Cathedral. I had no contacts there and did not even know the name of the Dean. As the first step I invited the Reverend Dr Martin Israel to see the picture and to meet Berthe Hess. We all lunched together and Martin felt that the picture was inspired by God. I then called on Dean Webster of St Paul's without an appointment and persuaded him to come with me to see the picture. He was not too happy about the idea of the picture being unveiled in St Paul's: 'We have to be very careful.' I mentioned that Dr Martin Israel felt that the picture was inspired. The effect was dramatic. 'Martin Israel!' exclaimed Dean Webster and the picture was duly unveiled in the Cathedral by the Dean, assisted by the Reverend Dr Martin Israel, in May 1984. This was Christian Heritage Year and Berthe loaned me the picture for our Christian Staircase Pilgrimage which we formed at Loseley that year. The original picture is of built-up oil paint and weighs over half a hundredweight. Unfortunately it does not reproduce well but it is included in the picture section of this book. We have a full-sized reproduction in our Chapel Vestry Hall at Loseley, the Thomas More Room.

Soon after my first visit to Crowhurst, I attended a meeting addressed by David Payne at Normanhurst, the Godalming home of Roger and Peggy de Pemberton. As a result of that meeting I became a founder member of the Godalming Guild of Health Prayer Group, led by Peggy at Normanhurst, with Roger, Dr Chris Jagger, a local GP, and six other lay Christians. Chris and his wife Maggie are very active Christians and Chris had a number of patients who were not being healed medically but were greatly helped by prayer. I kept a note of the patients who came to our fortnightly evenings and there were only three out of sixty who did not appear to receive any benefit at all. We had just one patient each evening, with their spouse if they wished. At 8.30 p.m. the members met for a half-hour briefing about the patient, preparation, prayer and sometimes meditation.

At 9 p.m. the patient came and was asked to tell us about their problems, to be treated in complete confidence. We gave advice, which might be to see their solicitor or bank manager, to change their diet or whatever appeared to be helpful in their situation. We then offered prayer, which was always accepted, and then the laying on of hands with prayer. The evening ended with a relaxing cup of coffee at about 10 p.m.

Problems brought to us included marriage breakdowns, cancer, various forms of physical and emotional ill health, resentments, stress and worry and an occult haunting etc. The haunting had been caused by past occult practices at a property before the occupation by the present owners, who had suffered distress and fear from the occurrences. Our meeting with them happened to coincide with the attendance of Bishop Morris and Anne Maddocks. We were all aware of an evil occult atmosphere and many, especially Anne Maddocks, felt extremely hot and uncomfortable. A separate team was praying for protection in another room. One of our members, Tom, a landscape gardener, has special gifts of healing, particularly in the field of the occult. He is one of a number of people I know who was offered to God by his mother before he was born. As in the other cases, the gift of Tom was accepted by God and he was given exceptional powers of divination and healing. He could discern evil spirits and it was Tom who led our prayers that night. It was not an experience that any of us would wish to repeat, but the battle was won.

Our first meeting with Bishop Maddocks and his wife Anne, a few years earlier, had proved another significant milestone in my Christian journey. At a garden picnic, following a funeral, Sue and I had met a wonderful man, Sir Ronald Harris, then Chief Church Commissioner, and his wife. Shortly afterwards they invited us to dine with them and the only other guests were Bishop Morris Maddocks and

Anne. The bishop had very recently resigned as Bishop of Selby to take on the unpaid position as Advisor to the Archbishops on the Church's ministry of healing. The Acorn Christian Healing Trust was being formed to support the bishop and his wife in the work to which they felt called, the spreading of the Christian healing ministry throughout the churches and the development of close harmony and understanding with the medical profession. Fortunately, I had just read the bishop's book *The Christian Healing Ministry* and was able to convey my keen interest in the subject and my thorough grasp of the book. Shortly afterwards, Dr Chris Jagger and I were invited to represent Guildford Diocese as founder-members of the Acorn Christian Healing Trust Apostolate. Apostolate pairs usually consist of one clergy or lay church member of any denomination and one member of the medical profession. There is an annual two-day Acorn conference and I have attended the first sixteen. The conference sessions are wide-ranging and include Bible study and at least two daily services and, latterly, a late night vigil. As usual at conferences, one of the benefits is the opportunity of sharing experiences and problems at mealtimes and outside the conference sessions with others working in this ministry. Sadly, many members do still have difficulty in getting the support of their clergy in developing the healing ministry in their parish.

Many people have the notion that God exists only in the minds of monks and nuns, bishops, priests, theologians and the lonely maiden aunt, and that real people have their lives to get on with. Yet God is there, however crowded life may be, however stressed, however full of temptation; in all these situations He is needed and He is available. It is at these times of anxiety, stress and problems that many people have discovered the reality of God. I am one of them.

I met a young woman in a Christian community who was

brought up in a loving Christian home. At the age of eighteen she got into bad company, ceased going to church, ceased to believe in God. Her life centred on alcohol, drugs and promiscuity on a hectic scale. One of her lovers died from drug abuse and in her shock and desolation she found God at a much deeper level than ever before and gave her life to Him. This kind of experience is more common than is realised.

Of course, not all people come to God because of problems. The Mother General of the Sisters of St Francis and the Divine Motherhood once told me that she asked a girl, who had applied to join the Order as a novice, why she wanted to be a nun. The reply came back: 'If there is a God I can think of nothing better than serving Him. If there is not, I shall never know!' Perhaps not the most inspired motive for becoming a nun, but a very practical response. We human beings are all different and we are called to serve in different ways in accordance with our particular gifts. Even within the Church we are apt to expect people to think and act as we ourselves do and we tend to be critical if they do things differently or do not fit in with our own ideas. Our Lord's injunction: 'Do not judge, and you will not be judged' (Matthew 7:1) is too often forgotten.

St Paul himself mentioned the gifts of the Spirit (1 Corinthians 12:7-11). The gifts of wise speech, faith, healing, miraculous powers, prophecy, ability to distinguish true spirits from false, the gift of tongues of various kinds and of interpretation of tongues – all these gifts are the activity of one and the same Spirit, who distributes them to each individual at will. Apart from the gifts of the Spirit, there are other natural gifts, as diverse as artistic or musical talents, craftsmanship and hospitality, which we are able to use in God's service. We have considered the emphasis placed by Jesus on love, God's greatest gift, and love is what He most desires from us. This point is also made by St Paul in the well-known passage 1 Corinthians 13. 'I may speak in tongues of men or of angels, but if I have no love, I am a sounding gong or a clanging cymbal . . . I may have faith enough to move mountains; but if I have no love, I am nothing. I may give all I possess to the needy, I may give my body to be burnt, but if I have no love, I gain nothing by it.' Our Lord emphasised that to love is the greatest of the commandments – first love the Lord thy God and second, love thy neighbour. On these two commandments hang all the law and the prophets. I am aware that this is the guts of the whole business – love. It gets trampled under the morass of theology, forms of liturgy, services and denominations and arguments about women priests, quite apart from all the delights and temptations of modern secular life with its emphasis on personal wealth and power. All of these are obscuring spirituality. Christianity is about love and if those of us who call ourselves Christians could remember that and really live it, then the churches will become truly alive.

When I first experienced the reality of God, in 1958, the first thing that God had shown me was His love . . . and then His glory. Until that moment I had been aware that I was commanded to love Him and I did so with a sense of duty, but it is not easy to continue to really love someone unless you feel that they also love you. I knew from the Bible that He did love me but somehow it was a love that was dutiful and respectful rather than passionate. From the instant of feeling His love flowing into me, I knew it was real and then I was able to respond with the warmth that He needed from me. Some eighteen years after that 1958 experience, I made a dedication to God and He responded. Through the power of His Holy Spirit He commissioned me to convey His love to the sick and suffering and led me to minister to cancer patients.

To put things in proper perspective, I should mention that during these years I had a hectic business life with farming and the estate and an expanding home manufacturing company, Guildway, which had persistent financial problems. My wife Sue was also fully stretched with the House open to the public. For most of the post-war period I wrote a note of what I had done each day and, looking back, I am amazed at the number of meetings and the variety of work that I got through. I do not know how I managed to fit in all the Christian bits, which gradually increased, but I thank God that I did. These are what matter most to me now! Being a Christian does not imply weakness but, on the contrary, strength and high standards. Compassion also, of course, and this is the way in which one can serve in business as a Christian. Christian compassion, caring and prayer provide a practical Christian witness for people who are very ill, those with serious problems, the dying and the bereaved. Harry, the young Guildway mechanic mentioned earlier in this chapter, is an example, though I have always regretted that greater glory was not given to God for his period of remission.

I soon discovered, both at Guildway and on the farm, that the boss or any executive cannot evangelise satisfactorily in his own business. The vital thing is that he should set an example in being straightforward, fair, honest and compassionate. This is much more rewarding and builds a much better reputation than single-minded pursuit of profit. Of course, profit is essential for survival but it is not where the true riches are to be found.

Michael, a prominent local Christian, became a non-executive director of my company. He had had a successful career in property and became chairman of a well-known public company. He was a Baptist, having been an elder of the Guildford Millmead Church and it was he who introduced me to the Full Gospel Businessmen's Fellowship International in which he held high office, later going on to spearhead important overseas Christian initiatives. We went on a number of retreats together in earlier days. Michael had become a Christian during his business career and made up for lost time by the energy and dedication which he put into his Christian work. He had a powerful gift of discernment, but towards the end of my business career, I failed to respond when Michael told me that he felt the Lord might be leading him to take over from me as chairman of Guildway. It seemed a preposterous suggestion. I had appointed Michael as a non-executive director of the company but he had no experience of manufacturing and Guildway was very specialised. I had formed the company in 1947 and had been dedicated to it ever since. It was significant to me that through the company I had come to experience God at a much deeper level. I also knew that my fellow directors would not be happy with my relinquishing the chairmanship to Michael.

I am featuring this episode because it raises important questions for Christians involved in business management. I might have been guided that it was the Lord's will that we should liquidate the company and sell the site. We would have raised a large sum, allowing very generous redundancy payments to all members of the firm. In material terms, Loseley would have received a considerable sum, which would have greatly helped the development of our dairy and organic projects, ensuring long-term survival of the estate. Also very significant, the Loseley Christian Trust and the Loseley and Guildway Charitable Trust owned between them 40 per cent of the Guildway shares, so would have benefited enormously, free of tax. The timber-frame housing industry had been going through a very difficult time, but I was determined to keep going. Guildway had brought me closer to God. I had a deep commitment to the company and all who worked in it. Eventually we did manage to sell Guildway as a going concern, but for a small fraction of the land value. The new owner did not share my ideals and all who worked at Guildway said: 'It is not the same.' The Honorary Chaplain was dropped. The company changed hands three times in ten years and finally just ceased to exist.

We do have these Christian dilemmas. I had considered that I was keeping faith with my ideals, but Christians need to make time and space for prayer and discernment as well as for open discussion. If I had said to Michael: 'Let's talk and pray about it,' we might have felt led that on this occasion it was not the Lord's will for us to keep the company going at all costs. We cannot always be certain of knowing God's will; we should not make assumptions about big decisions without making time for prayer and 'waiting upon God' for guidance. I had kept faith with my ideals, but I did not stay close enough to God.

St Francis has long been an influence in my life. He had been born rich but after an exuberant, playboy youth, he gave away all his possessions and dedicated his life to God. St Francis regarded all animals, and indeed all of Creation, as his brothers and sisters and he loved them all. He would never have approved of exploitation or cruelty. Cruelty to animals has always deeply concerned me. It is not a subject that appears to have received condemnation in the New Testament but we have St Francis for an example and he was very close to God and revered as a saint in his lifetime. I have mentioned my association with the Roman Catholic Sisters of St Francis and the Divine Motherhood. Also near us is the Franciscan Friary, the Order of Friars Minor, at Chilworth. I frequently have the privilege of attending the Mass there and having meals with the brothers. A considerable portion of this book has been written on visits to this hospitable friary and it was the words of the learned Father Ignatius OFM that inspired the title. The previous Guardian (Governor) of the friary, Brother Jo, in his final year before leaving for Thailand to help the terminally ill, cycled on a sponsored ride from Surrey to Rome via Assisi and back, seventy miles a day, sometimes through snow. It was a splendid effort and Jo did admit that there were times when he wept with pain and exhaustion. The friary also serves as one of the local Catholic churches and Jo's successor as Governor is Brother Juniper who is the Roman Catholic priest for the area.

St Francis founded a Third Order for lay people and I was accepted by the Anglican Third Order as a postulate and then as a novice. This entailed keeping rules, including minimum set times of prayer and Christian work, as well as attendance at meetings and services of worship. There were helpful talks from Franciscan monks and lay members from other dioceses and we had occasional visits to Franciscan friaries and convents. Each branch has a novice counsellor and a chaplain and members are required to have a spiritual director with whom they meet quarterly, which includes the opportunity for confession. I learned a great deal more about the blessed Francis, the disciplines were helpful and constructive and the services uplifting. I felt in harmony with the other members and made new friends with similar ideals to my own. Everything was fine but for me there were two problems. The friars and nuns of the Order take a vow of poverty, chastity and obedience. I believe poverty and simplicity to be significant, but as chairman of a company and with official duties in the county, I could not go about in simple garb, without a tie and using public transport in preference to a car, as was encouraged for members of the Third Order. If I took Sue out to a good restaurant for dinner, I had a feeling of guilt. I was also getting over-active. Apart from a hectic business life, I was also involved in many Christian activities including the Acorn Christian Healing Trust, Compton Parish, St Francis, Littleton, two other prayer groups, visiting sick people and a number of voluntary secular activities including, at that time, the management committee of the local Cheshire Home. On occasion I did manage to fit in three meetings in an evening, but something had to go. Following my two years as a Franciscan novice, I was due to be professed as a full member. After prayer and careful consideration, I reluctantly decided that I must leave. I still keep many of the Franciscan rules, including a daily half-hour prayer time. I revere St Francis as much as ever and continue to value the friendships made. My time in the Third Order represents a significant stage in my Christian journey.

Sue had not felt led to join the Third Order and there were not many married couples in membership together. We are not all called in the same direction, we do not all have the same gifts and there will always be the Marthas, who do the practical work, and the Marys who make time to pray. Sue and I attend church together and we are alike in our Anglican churchmanship. She had not shared my experience of God on that June evening in 1958 and from then on I felt a deeper need to attend Christian spiritual gatherings to which Sue did not feel drawn. I completely understood the situation, with a humility bordering on guilt. I also deeply appreciated that Sue never complained or tried to prevent me going off to these meetings, though sometimes I know that it was painful for her. Patience and love triumph and we were eventually blessed by being led together to a very fulfilling and compassionate Christian ministry.

Chapter 5

LOVE

Love: this wonderful word is rapidly losing its true meaning and now encompasses false glamour, sex and selfishness. True love is so different and this is the love at the heart of Christianity. If more people realised this they might not write off religion as 'dull'.

Jesus reminds us that the first commandment is to love. 'Love the Lord your God with all your heart, with all your mind, with all your soul and with all your strength.' And the second commandment flows from it: to 'love your neighbour as yourself.' We are also taught that God loves each one of us. Love needs to be experienced as well as being spoken and I suspect that I am not the only Christian to admit that my love of God was originally a dutiful love and not passionate. Of course, I should have prayed to be able to love Him at a deeper level, but it never occurred to me to do so. Fortunately, God was aware that I believed in Him and He knew that, not being aware of the depth of His love, I was unable to respond.

The situation changed dramatically when God poured His love into my head, as described in Chapter 3. I feel it is significant that within about twenty minutes that evening I received three great gifts of enhanced awareness of God. The first was of His love. When I commenced to pray I received awareness of His presence. I immediately responded by falling on my knees and then I was flooded with the light of His glory. Only on writing this does the realisation come to me that if I had received only awareness of God's love, I could later have doubted if it really had come from God. But God had then made known to me His presence: without question He was there beside me. When I responded to that, by falling to my knees, the light of His glory was intense. I had received His passionate love, followed by an awareness that God was there with me and then I beheld His glory. Of course, my faith was multiplied but the really important gift was the reality of the love of God for me. From that moment it became so easy to respond to that love, though it is never possible to respond adequately. I knew that He wanted me to serve Him, but He was not telling me anything about that then, or for some time to come. He knew, and gradually I knew, that I had much to learn and I was gradually made aware of how to set about this preparation. That experience took place just after my thirty-eighth birthday and from then on I have tried to respond to God's love by serving Him in accordance with His will. The best way of showing love for someone is by helping them in any way we can. I am very aware that my efforts are feeble and inadequate, but the intention is there and the motivation is love. It is always helpful if the beloved makes known their wants, so that one can respond. God does do that. Jesus taught us the Father's likes and dislikes. Love, worship and glorify Him. Help the poor, the sick and the needy. Apart from general needs of this nature, I have received a number of 'nudges' from God, an awareness of things to do that would please Him. I have felt clearly led to a number of Loseley initiatives in the Christian cause including the Christian staircase, the chapels, the Christian Trust, the picture of The Living Christ, involvement in the healing ministry, Christian cancer care and finally, the writing of this book.

To prove their love for God, each Christian must strive every day to do His will. Often it is instinctive: we know well enough His commandments, and His Son's teaching, and we do our best to comply. If we fail we know that God is hurt and we need to confess our transgressions in penitence and resolve to do better in future. If we are not concerned about disobeying and hurting the One we love, then our love is meaningless.

Just a month before writing this chapter I received a book, *Why God?* by the Bishop of Bath and Wells, Jim Thompson. The bishop opens his introduction with the words: 'The greatest day of my life was the day I discovered that God loved me – not only that He existed but that He loved me.' The paragraph ends: 'Once you have been blessed by the love of God, it's very hard to keep quiet about it. So I'm still rattling on some thirty years after the event.' And so am I, nearly forty-two years after my event! Love is a wondrous thing and very precious, but above all love is the love of God.

Mary is the name of three women, abounding in love, who featured in our Lord's life. First, Mary His mother. What obedience, what love and what terrible suffering. Mary was aware of the ignominy she would suffer at being with child before marriage. She would also find her condition impossible to explain to Joseph to whom she was betrothed. In those days women who strayed were harshly treated and those caught in adultery were stoned to death. Many of us have seen the cave in the Church of the Annunciation at Nazareth where the Angel Gabriel appeared to Mary and told her that she would bear a son, fathered by the Holy Spirit. Mary's response was: 'Be it unto me according to thy word.' Joseph proposed to set aside the marriage contract but in a dream he had a vision of an angel telling him not to be afraid to take Mary to be his wife and that the Holy Spirit was the father of the child to be born, to be named Jesus. Joseph obeyed but Mary's troubles were far from over. There was the journey to Bethlehem just before the birth was due and then the birth in the cattle shed. Less than three weeks later came the flight to Egypt with the babe Jesus. As Jesus grew up there must have been many tensions. It is recorded that when Jesus was twelve years old He went missing on the return from a visit to Jerusalem. Mary and Joseph had agonising days searching for Him, eventually finding Him in conversation with the learned rabbis in the temple. It was Mary who, at the marriage feast at Cana, told the servants to do what Jesus told them. This led to the first recorded miracle, turning the water into excellent wine. After His baptism by John in the River Jordan, Jesus left home and when He did return to visit Nazareth He was rejected and narrowly missed being stoned. Again, one can imagine His mother's feelings.

The next significant mention of Mary in the New Testament is at the crucifixion. It is hard to imagine greater anguish than seeing one's own son being crucified, made worse, if it is possible, by the knowledge that He was innocent. She remained close to the cross and Jesus placed her in the care of St John, 'the disciple that Jesus loved'. We know that St John lived to a great age and did have Mary with him at Ephesus and, for a time, on the Isle of Patmos. The death of Mary is not recorded, but her devotion to Jesus her son was divine and she has made appearances through the centuries and in various parts of the world. The visionaries have usually been simple peasant children and the Virgin has been appearing for several years and is still active at the start of the new millennium at Medjugorje, in Croatia. Millions have made the pilgrimage, including several of our friends, who have all been impressed with the atmosphere of deep spirituality. Many have returned several times. I wholeheartedly share the Roman Catholic veneration for the Blessed Virgin Mary. The Anglo-Catholics also revere her, but I can imagine the reaction if I had proposed to the PCC of St Nicholas Church, Compton that we should have a figure of the Madonna in the sanctuary! In my younger days

I was brought up to consider figures of the Madonna and the reverence shown by the Catholics for our Lady to be strange and 'not for us'. Not many Anglicans are aware of, or take seriously the appearances of our Lady. These are not approved by the Vatican until they have been very thoroughly researched and the visionaries are put through very rigorous investigation. A number of them have achieved sainthood. That is good enough for me and I consider that the attested miracles performed by the Virgin Mary for the love and honour of her Son are truly significant and should be better publicised. The Virgin Mary did not take these initiatives just for the sake of the visionaries, who had a most difficult task, but the messages are for all humankind. Mary is the mother of Jesus. She was selected by God, through the agency of the Angel Gabriel, as the one worthy to be mother to God's Son, full of obedience, love and reverence. Thank God for her.

Mary seems to have been the name associated with love in our Lord's ministry. We read in Luke 10:39-42 that:

> . . . she [Martha] had a sister, Mary, who seated herself at the Lord's feet and stayed there listening to his words . . . Martha . . . came to him and said, 'Lord, do you not care that my sister has left me to get on with the work by myself? Tell her to come and give me a hand.' But the Lord answered, 'Martha, Martha, you are fretting and fussing about so many things; only one thing is necessary. Mary has chosen what is best; it shall not be taken away from her.'

There is clear teaching here on the greater importance of Mary's love and of caring about people. We learn from John 11:2 that it was the same Mary who, on another occasion, presented Jesus with costly oil and washed His feet with her tears. The people present, including Judas, complained that the ointment should have been sold and the money given to the poor but Jesus again stood up for Mary, saying that the ointment was for His body after burial, also that His host had not washed His feet but: 'This woman has made my feet wet with her tears and wiped them with her hair. You gave me no kiss; but she has been kissing my feet ever since I came in . . . her great love proves that her many sins have been forgiven; where little has been forgiven, little love is shown.' I was glad to read again this passage from Luke 7:37–50. Once more, our Lord emphasised the importance of love. We do need to remind ourselves of this; we are often too quick in condemning people who overflow with love rather than assisting them to channel that love in the right direction.

We now come on to the third Mary, brimming with love, and few people can fail to have heard of St Mary of Magdala. She holds a unique place in the New Testament. Mary, at dawn on the first day of the week, was first at the tomb, discovered it was empty and told the disciples. Again, it was Mary Magdalene who was the first to see our Lord after His resurrection on the third day. Jesus entrusted her with a message for the disciples: 'Go and take the word to my brothers that they are to leave for Galilee.' 'I have seen the Lord' she blurted out and gave this message (John 20:18). Those five simple words form possibly the most dramatic statement ever made. Just imagine those disillusioned, dejected, frightened disciples. All had been lost and the Lord, who they had believed to be the Messiah, had been crucified. Now Mary was telling them that He was alive, she had seen Him and they were to go and rejoin Him. It is worth spending time reflecting on that scene.

There are theories that Mary Magdalene had been a woman of ill repute, but there seems to be nothing in the scriptures to substantiate this, although Mark (16:9), recording that our Lord first appeared to Mary Magdalene, adds: 'From whom He had driven out seven demons' (see also Luke 8:2). Magdala is in Galilee and this healing would have taken place earlier in our Lord's ministry there. As in other cases, Mary had received our Lord's healing and dedicated her life to Him. Many of us have been privileged to receive God's healing; are we prepared to follow Mary's example? The Gospels show that Mary Magdalene was a loving and passionate person by nature. I often recollect a sermon given by a bishop in Westminster Abbey on the day of the Feast of the Presentation of Jesus in the Temple. The theme of the sermon was that anything offered to God becomes holy. That is a very powerful thought and, although the preacher did not mention her, Mary Magdalene is a perfect example. Mary offered her love to God and that love was transformed, became holy and spiritual, leading to a role in which she was blessed beyond measure.

In the example of Mary Magdalene there is hope and glorious opportunity for all those whose love has been shattered through desertion or bereavement. I do not underestimate the pain and horror of these situations and we all know people who have been desperately hurt and wounded, sometimes irreparably, through divorce. The trauma, the tears, the recriminations, feelings of guilt, bitterness and times of despair sometimes eventually lead to a frantic search for new love or to a hardening, a setting up of a barrier against any close friendship for fear of further hurt. Thankfully there is a way forward, even in the most hurtful situation. We can follow the example of St Mary of Magdala and offer our love to God. God will always readily accept it. Love is the most precious and valued gift that we can offer and in making the offering to God our love is transformed by Him into a powerful spiritual love, a love which God can use to transform and to heal. Anything given to God becomes holy. Many of us have met people who have triumphed over their adversities in this way, by offering their love to God. They are the sort of people who radiate peace and love but would not wish to discuss their experiences. In the Christian healing ministry we meet people who receive great blessings from God, sometimes in response to love surrendered to Him. God needs our love, so that it can be poured out to comfort and heal the sick, the suffering and the lost.

In this chapter we are considering the supreme importance of love. Our love of God is our response to His immeasurable love for us. In God's commandments we are instructed also to love our neighbour, implying everyone. Our Lord made another significant statement about love: 'Love one another, as I have loved you. There is no greater love than this, that a man should lay down his life for his friends.' He Himself did no less than lay down His life for all mankind. How can we respond, except with love? We have considered Mary Magdalene. Her example has been followed, not only by many whose human love has been rejected but by hundreds of thousands of men and women who have taken a vow of celibacy as Catholic priests and monks and nuns. What a tremendous commitment and what a sacrifice! It makes one feel very inadequate. I personally feel called to God's service, but have never felt called to priesthood or monasticism. I do revere those who are obedient to such a call. It is a measure of the degree of love for God shown by the religious that some are prepared to live their lives in strict obedience to the rules of chastity and poverty and obedience. The influence and example of the religious Orders becomes increasingly important as our world, obsessed with selfishness, sex and possessions, moves further away from God. Many of us lay people have been richly blessed through the friendship and guidance of monks and nuns and we are most grateful to them. More might take advantage of retreats and quiet days, conducted by members of these Orders, if they were aware of them.

Although giving their love to God, it is understandable that for some monks and nuns the strain of total physical abstinence is too great. There are occasions of scandal, seized upon with glee and blown up by the gutter press. Sue and I did try to help a monk, a revered friend, who was not guilty but framed and driven almost insane by the press. I mention this because, although monks and nuns are generally revered, one does meet people who, in ignorance, think of them as merely opting out of life. Nothing could be further from the truth. It would be more appropriate to say that many of the rest of us are opting out of God.

In this chapter we have considered God's love for us. We have dwelt on the love of Mary, mother of Jesus, her tribulations, sorrows and continuing work for God; Mary, sister of Martha, whose loving nature was commended by Jesus; and St Mary of Magdala, who gave her life to God, an example for all of us, especially those whose love is abused or spurned. More important in today's world than ever is the example of the religious Orders dedicated to loving service to God and vowed to chastity, poverty and obedience.

The final testimony of love in this chapter is a situation in which Sue and I were privileged to be involved. One day, Joan, a staff member, asked to see me and this is what she had to say – her sister Kit and brother-in-law John, who lived in Wales, had been married for some twenty years and had been unable to have a child. At last, when they had almost given up hope, a daughter was born. There was great rejoicing and thanksgiving and a christening service attended by all their friends. A few months later it was apparent that something was terribly wrong. Harriet had a rare and fatal condition, known as Leigh's encephalopathy. I telephoned a well-known Christian pathologist for advice as to whether to pray for healing or reconciliation. 'Reconciliation' was the immediate response, 'there is no known case of survival beyond four years'. I gave this sad news to Joan, but she responded: 'I'm praying for healing.' 'And so will I,' I said.

A few days later I went up to meet Kit and John and Harriet for the first time, at the Great Ormond Street Childrens' Hospital. 'We know that Harriet has not long to live,' said Kit, 'but we would love to have her at home for her last few weeks'. We prayed together and then I went to the ward with John and prayed over Harriet. She was lying in a cot, tiny, helpless and adorable. She was just a few months old, the most precious, adored gift her parents had ever received, and with a life expectancy only of months. Harriet's condition meant that she would never be able to do anything for herself; she would never speak, stand, walk, turn herself over in bed or use her hands. She would need attention twenty-four hours a day.

It is appropriate to pause just for a moment and dwell on that situation. It was an obvious breeding ground for bitterness, resentment, or recrimination. Why did God allow it? How could He be so cruel? Why? Why? Why? But it was not a bit like that. Harriet is a glorious tale of triumph over disaster and the catalyst that made it so is clear for all to see: the one word LOVE.

Kit had immediately given up her job teaching handicapped children and John went part-time in his job. Harriet was transferred from Great Ormond Street to the Neville Hall Hospital, Abergavenny, not many miles from their home at Llangynidr. She was allowed home for a short spell. Kit and John managed so well that the home visits were extended, with short spells in hospital as needed. No one who saw Harriet could fail to be charmed by her. She seemed to be absorbing and radiating the great flood of love that she was receiving. She had no control of her limbs and she could not speak, but Harriet made up for all this with her glorious smile. This was unique and a very special method of communication.

The friends and neighbours rallied round magnificently.

A Harriet Davis Supporters Club was formed and raised over £70,000 for the Research Trust for Metabolic Diseases in Children, to assist with providing special equipment for Harriet. It also eventually raised £130,000 towards the Harriet Davis Seaside Holiday Trust, which now provides seaside holiday accommodation at Tenby on the Welsh coast in two houses specially equipped for children with similar problems to Harriet. Sue and I are privileged to be vice patrons of the Trust and we attended the very moving opening of the first home, known as Harriet's House, by the Bishop of Swansea. Harriet loved her trips to the sea and Kit and John knew that she would have rejoiced in being able to help so many other children with disabilities to enjoy a seaside holiday.

Kit and John had developed a method of communicating which used an electronic board containing the alphabet and various pictures. They would ask Harriet a question, for instance: 'Are you hungry?' They would hold her arm and sense the letters she wanted pressed and move her hand accordingly. We are witnesses to the fact that it did work and Harriet's brain was kept active. In the past, any child unable to speak or express themselves was considered to be an imbecile and no determined efforts were made to achieve communication. Harriet was taught about Jesus and it was a very special day when, aged ten, she was confirmed by the Bishop of Swansea. Sue and I visited the family at Llangynidr most years and it was a great day for us when Harriet, Kit and John came to see us and we spent some time together in the chapel.

The experts had given a maximum life expectancy of four years, but Harriet was eleven when she died. She lives on in the minds of all who met her. Few people can have generated so much love and compassion in a lifetime; tremendous credit is due to her parents, the support team, led by her doctor, Sandy Cavenagh, and the specialists and nurses of the two hospitals. One of them has stated in print: 'Her illness and life have made at least one not very Christian practitioner ponder anew the meaning of immortality.' It surely calls us all to ponder anew the full meaning of love.

Whatever the meaning of love, it is at the heart of God, and in the next chapter we turn our thoughts to the Almighty God, the Three in One.

Chapter 6

THREE IN ONE

I am not a theologian or a scholar and I am not qualified to teach. People find it hard to understand how God can be Three In One. This chapter represents my own personal understanding, in the final years of my life, as a dedicated lay Christian. Years ago, Sue and I listened to a sermon on the subject by a learned theologian. I remember saying, as we drove home: 'If we have to understand *that* to be Christians, there is no hope!' Years later I was suddenly given the realisation that it is quite simple:

- God the Father, the Creator, is also Jehovah, the God of the Jews.
- God the Father and God the Son existed before the creation of the world.
- God the Son, Jesus Christ, came to earth in human form, fathered by the Holy Spirit and born of Mary, a virgin (Luke 1:26–38). The Angel Gabriel visited Mary and told her that she was to conceive and give birth to a son: 'and you are to give him the name Jesus.' Mary queried how this could be as she was still a virgin. The angel answered: 'The Holy Spirit will come upon you, and the power of the Most High will overshadow you; for that reason the holy child to be born will be called Son of God.' Mary responded: 'I am the Lord's servant, may it be as you have said.'
- The third member of the Trinity, the Holy Spirit, is the

Spirit of God and now God's link with the world. The Holy Spirit fell upon Jesus 'like a dove' at His baptism. After His crucifixion and resurrection and before ascending into Heaven, Jesus told the disciples that the Father would soon send the Holy Spirit to them. This happened some ten days later, on the day of Pentecost. The Holy Spirit continues to be very active in our own times.

- God the Father and God the Son, now ascended, remain in Heaven and are One with the Holy Spirit, who represents them on earth and is always available to us if we open ourselves to Him. Our Lord stated: 'God is spirit, and those who worship him must worship in spirit and in truth' (John 4:24). When we talk about God's love, it is the love of Father, Son and Holy Spirit, united in one spirit. This in no way conflicts with our personal daily relationship with Jesus.

Of course, we mortals cannot expect fully to comprehend God. He is further above us than we are above insect life, but we do need to have an understanding of the nature of the God whom we love and worship. God is spirit but Jesus himself spent some thirty-four years as a human being on this earth. We can channel our prayers, our praise and our thoughts through Him or through the Father or the Holy Spirit. They are One, in perfect union. It is not necessary for us to understand the exact nature of God. All things are possible for God, the Creator. There are arrogant and too-clever humans who are unable to believe in God because they consider that this or that is not possible. We must accept the holy Scriptures and the fact is that those who accept Him, love Him, worship and obey Him do experience the reality of the love and power of Almighty God. That is a gift beyond price.

Many people are surprised to learn that human beings are

also three in one, but it is a fact that we are body, mind and emotions, and spirit. All these components need to be kept in healthy condition if we are to be truly fit and 'whole'. Wholeness is a term often used in the Christian healing ministry and it is a fact that unless our spiritual relationship with God is healthy, we are incomplete and not whole. These three components are interdependent. If we are not well in our body, our mind cannot function effectively and if our mind is unsound we shall be unable to keep our body in good shape. If our spiritual life is unsound it can cause guilt, which will affect both our mental and physical health. We need to be well in body, mind and spirit; that is wholeness, and without God we are not whole. Sadly, so many people suffer from being unaware that they have a spiritual dimension.

Obviously some individuals, such as Olympic athletes, are better endowed physically than others, while some, such as professors and brilliant philosophers and mathematicians, are mentally superior, and others, potential saints, mystics and members of religious orders are very spiritual but may lack physical strength. There is a lot to be said for being 'rounded'. A professor will probably be more clear-headed if he takes some exercise and those of us who are less mentally gifted need to 'use our think', as an old countryman aptly put it, if we are to live a full life. Long before he became a bishop, David Shepherd played cricket for England and never dropped his interest or support for the game and there are Olympic athletes who are evangelists and all the more effective because of their sporting reputations.

The third element is the soul, the spiritual. This is implanted in all people and is potentially more important than body and mind as it is the part of us that goes on to the eternal. Every human being is born with a spark of God within. Sadly, many people are not aware of the spiritual element, though most at some time experience a feeling that there is 'something'. Our spiritual nature lies dormant, but available to be kindled and it is a thrilling moment when this happens. The spark can come through a vision, the glimpse of an angel, a personal experience of God, voices, as in the case of Joan of Arc, music, or in a deep silence. It can be dramatic and instant or a gradual dawning. Usually the ignition of the spiritual spark comes through another human being who at the time may be quite unaware of the vital part they are playing in bringing about this spiritual awakening in someone. I was once told, by a person I did not even recognise, that long ago my prayer had saved his life. There is a line about entertaining angels unawares and we should, as it were, have the kettle ready on the hob for them.

Understandably, people are more aware of their material nature than of the spiritual. 'We're in this world now,' is a common response when spiritual matters are mentioned. Yes, we are in this world and on the earth, but there is much more to life than that! We are called for a time to live a double life: our material existence on earth in preparation for our eternal life in God's Kingdom. For life on earth we are given the rules, in the form of the Ten Commandments, to keep us on the right track.

Some 2,000 years ago Jesus Christ, Son of God, came into the world to give us true awareness of God. He showed His divinity through His teaching and the miracles that He performed, particularly the many miracles of healing. Most vital of all, Jesus taught how we could achieve eternal life. Love is the key, love of God and love of our fellow beings: forgiveness, helping the poor and the lonely, the sick and the suffering and showing compassion for all in need. One might have expected that all humankind would have accepted and applauded this divine manifestation and teaching, leading to a near perfect world. Instead, the world of His day rejected Him, mocked Him, scourged Him and crucified Him. Yet, despite this, we were given another chance. Three days after Jesus was crucified, He rose from the dead and appeared to many. He showed the disciples the wounds of the crucifixion on His hands and feet and His pierced side. He stated to the apostle Thomas: 'Happy are they who find faith without seeing me' (John 20:29). That, I believe, clearly includes those of us today who do believe without having seen Him. Happy indeed we should be.

Jesus ascended into Heaven, first promising that when He returned to Heaven, God would send down the Holy Spirit. On the day of Pentecost, the Holy Spirit was sent and amazing spiritual gifts were given, including people speaking in new languages. The Holy Spirit today remains available to all who open themselves to God and pray to be filled with His Spirit. All over the world millions of people are experiencing the power of the Holy Spirit. Jesus, when on earth, healed those who came and asked for healing – the sick, the lame, the blind, the deaf and the dumb. All were healed by God's power. After Jesus had left them and ascended into Heaven, the disciples continued the healing ministry which they had learned through Jesus. We read in Acts 5: 'all were cured.'

Like Jesus in the days of His ministry, the disciples were 'in this world'. Like Jesus, they believed, they prayed to God and they were empowered by the Holy Spirit. They were obedient to the teaching of Jesus and they knew that they must serve God and do His will, even though it was a life of hardship and danger, which led to many of them being put to death as martyrs.

After our Lord's crucifixion, one of the most ardent persecutors of the Christians was a brilliant and well-educated man named Saul. To the amazement and dismay of his fellow Jews, Saul was miraculously converted when about to enter Damascus to persecute the Christians there. Saul, re-named Paul, joined the apostles and became the most effective servant of the Lord in teaching, preaching and healing in the name of Jesus (Acts 9:1–22). The Christian Church was established and gradually grew in all the corners of the earth. The Church grew because the disciples followed the teaching and example of Jesus – healing the sick in the name of God, demonstrating the reality of His power and proclaiming the Kingdom of Heaven. They were very aware of the importance of the Holy Spirit. An unstoppable combination: promise of eternal life to come and demonstration of the reality of God's power to heal on earth. The underlying teaching was unchanging: love and forgiveness. Love God and give Him the glory and show love to your fellow humans by active compassion for those in need.

How fortunate and privileged we are to have our Lord's teaching recorded for us in the Gospels as well as accounts of the miracles of healing that He performed. In Acts are recorded the miracles and teaching of the apostles and Paul after our Lord's ascension. Many of us have had the privilege of visiting the sites in the Holy Land of Palestine where our Lord lived, taught and worked miracles. These sites are revered and magnificently maintained. Sites in Galilee such as the Mount of the Beatitudes and the shore of the lake where our Lord cooked the fish are completely unspoilt by man. Jesus really was there and we know what He said and did. Behind the altar of the Nazareth Church of The Annunciation the cave is still visible where the Angel Gabriel appeared to Mary. The garden tomb, discovered by General Gordon, is not yet confirmed as the tomb where our Lord was laid, but it fits perfectly with the description and the site is beautifully kept by the English Trustees.

If you truly love someone, you need to please them, need to be close to them and need to give to them. There is joyous satisfaction in growing closer together in harmonious love. So it is in our relationship with God and it is logical that His first request to us should have been for love. We respond to

His love by loving Him and by loving our fellow beings.

Those who wish for spiritual growth and the development of their spiritual dimension are well catered for through books, seminars, retreats and courses. Each of us needs to discover and deepen our own spirituality and to develop our relationship with Almighty God. We do need to discipline ourselves to make more time for God. Our Lord himself had to make a special effort to escape the crowds, by climbing the hills or going away in a boat, in order to be alone with the Father. We have to escape from the telephone, the doorbell and the pressures of modern life and it is worth the effort to get up half an hour early and give that time to God.

We need to remember that in the spirit world there is evil as well as good: God is not dead, but neither is the devil. Just as countless numbers in every age have discovered the reality of the power and the love of God, so many have found the reality of evil spirits in the occult. People have been driven to madness and suicide and some have become witches. I have met a former witch, who fortunately had been converted and is now a passionate Christian. I know of one English town where there are a number of active witches; the authorities refuse to take action against them, regarding them as 'religious'! There is increasing interest in the occult and dabbling in any area of this — ouija boards, planchette or any form of spiritualism — is forbidden and very dangerous. I have met people who have been driven to the verge of insanity by such involvement. The only way out is through exorcism by the power of the Holy Spirit and in every diocese there are ministers authorised and trained in this specialist ministry. It is important that such cases should be left in their hands or further serious complications can follow. I have witnessed people being delivered of evil spirits; it is not a pretty sight and very noisy.

Our friend and long-time chaplain the Reverend Pat

Ashe once very reluctantly attended a spiritualist séance at a party. Those present were told to put their hands on a glass tumbler placed on a table. Pat prayed to God that the Holy Spirit should be in charge and allow nothing to occur unless it was His will. Nothing did happen. 'Extraordinary,' cried the leader, 'something always happens.' Then there was a loud bang and nothing more. This was a clear case of the power of God triumphing over the occult.

As with many other things, there are degrees of evil and there are different views on the details. Horoscopes and fortune-telling are not horrendous but they are rightly frowned on by Christian authorities and they can cause problems. There are those who regard freemasons, water diviners and acupuncturists as allied to the devil and Bach flower remedies as being not much better. I am not alone in disagreeing and I definitely do not regard any of these as evil. I know many people who have been helped through acupuncture and a Chinese bishop assured me that the acupuncture available in this country has no religious significance. Surely it must be within God's will for a water diviner to make the desert fruitful. And if he first prayed to God for discernment and gave thanks afterwards, better still. This, I believe is the distinction. If constructive things are truly done with prayer and for God's glory, it is unlikely to be evil. The more we can offer to God the better and the more we pray regarding our tasks the more our work will be blessed.

The Holy Spirit was sent to us shortly after our Lord's ascension, on the day of Pentecost. In Old Testament times the Holy Spirit had only been in evidence when working through the Prophets. When our Lord ascended we were granted the presence of the Holy Spirit on earth and He is available to you and to me when we open ourselves to Him. He will guide us, grant us knowledge, empower us and work miracles of healing. He is part of Almighty God. One of the few things that I learned in my younger days about the Holy Spirit was that 'Every sin and every slander can be forgiven, except slander spoken against the Spirit; that will not be forgiven.' These are our Lord's words, in Matthew 12:31 (see also Mark 3:29 and Luke 12:10). This does need to be taken very seriously. The following passages in the New Testament give a background on the ways in which the Holy Spirit helps and guides those who are open to Him:

- Mark 13:11 – So when you are arrested and put on trial do not worry beforehand about what you will say, but when the time comes say whatever is given you to say, for it is not you who will be speaking, but the Holy Spirit.
- Luke 1:15 (speaking of the coming of John the Baptist, the angel tells Zechariah) – From his very birth he will be filled with the Holy Spirit.
- Luke 1:35 (the angel informs the Virgin Mary) – The Holy Spirit will come upon you, and the power of the Most High will overshadow you.
- Luke 2:25–26 – There was at that time in Jerusalem a man called Simeon . . . and the Holy Spirit was upon him. It had been revealed to him by the Holy Spirit that he would not see death until he had seen the Lord's Messiah. Guided by the Spirit he came into the temple . . . took him in his arms, praised God and said: 'Now, Lord, you are releasing your servant in peace, according to your promise.
- Luke 3:22 (at the baptism of Jesus) – The Holy Spirit descended on him in bodily form like a dove, and there came a voice from Heaven, 'You are my beloved Son; in you I delight.'
- Luke 4:1 – Full of the Holy Spirit, Jesus returned from the Jordan, and for forty days he wandered in the wilderness . . .
- Luke 11:13 – If you, bad as you are, know how to

give good things to your children, how much more will the Heavenly Father give the Holy Spirit to those who ask him!

- Luke 12:12 – When the time comes the Holy Spirit will instruct you what to say.
- John 14:26 In his farewell discourses our Lord says – But the Advocate, the Holy Spirit whom the Father will send in my name, will teach you everything and remind you of all that I have told you.
- John 20:22 On our Lord's first appearance to the disciples after his resurrection – Then he breathed on them, saying, 'Receive the Holy Spirit!'

In addition to these verses from the Gospels, there are no fewer than thirty-two references in Acts to the Holy Spirit (see Appendix 1). St Luke, the author, commences the book of Acts: 'In the first part of my work, Theophilus, I gave an account of all that Jesus did and taught from the beginning until the day when He was taken up to Heaven, after giving instructions through the Holy Spirit to the apostles whom he had chosen.' It is clear from Acts that the power of the Holy Spirit is of very great significance in guiding, empowering and healing.

I personally have never felt led to receive the gift of tongues which is one of the dramatic gifts of the Spirit. I have heard people speaking in tongues and also praying in tongues and I have heard others interpreting these strange sounds. I know they are authentic, just as they were on the day of Pentecost following the ascension. The power of the Spirit must not be misused. I was a guest at a Youth Club evening in Brighton when members went up one by one to receive the gift of tongues, a number giggling with embarrassment. I was the only person who declined to go up and I was disturbed at what was going on. It is not wrong to be prayed over to receive the Holy Spirit, but it must be done in solemn reverence.

Many Christian people do not understand the Holy Spirit and are nervous about Him, as if He were something 'creepy' and unconnected with the God they learned about in childhood. I would urge them to seek instruction, for they are missing out. There are many helpful books available and Alpha courses, among others, are also useful. Unfortunately, there are some who have received gifts of the Holy Spirit, including tongues, who tend to show off, rather than respecting it as a gift for use in humility, in God's service. People who do not possess the gift are understandably put off by such misuse. Gifts of the Spirit are given by God for use in His service. The power of the Holy Spirit can be transmitted through the laying on of hands for healing, whether or not the Christian who is ministering is praying aloud – the power comes through their hands as God's channel. In 1 Corinthians 12:7–11 St Paul describes the gifts of the Spirit:

> In each of us the Spirit is seen to be at work for some useful purpose. One, through the Spirit, has the gift of wise speech, while another, by the power of the same Spirit, can put the deepest knowledge into words. Another, by the same Spirit, is granted faith; another, by the one Spirit, gifts of healing, and another miraculous powers; another has the gift of prophecy, and another the ability to distinguish true spirits from false; yet another has the gift of tongues of various kinds, and another the ability to interpret them.

Today these same gifts are still given.

The fruits of the Spirit are listed in Galatians 5:22–23: 'Love, joy, peace, patience, kindness, goodness, fidelity, gentleness and self-control.'

I have, on a number of occasions, witnessed people being

'slain in the Spirit' when hands are laid on them, or when prayed over, in the standing position. The one prayed for falls backwards and nearly always there is someone ready to prevent them falling heavily. Most find it a refreshing experience and some are healed.

The Holy Spirit was vitally important to the disciples and we are very privileged that the Spirit is available to us. I have a diary entry that on 26th December 1969, as I happened to switch on the radio, the first words were: 'As St Paul found, in times of weakness, God's Holy Spirit is there to give strength. May we be open to the Spirit that we may receive that strength.'

It is clear that Paul and the disciples were very aware of the power of the Holy Spirit and depended on it. But where is the Holy Spirit in our days? Right in our midst, ready to guide us and empower us, just as in the days of the apostles and as our Lord promised. Any Christian who is open to God and truly wishes to receive the Holy Spirit for use in God's service can almost certainly receive it of they are open to God. It is an awesome gift. I will end with the words of Bernard of Clairvaux, born in 1091, about midway between the time of St Paul and today: 'Being infused with the Holy Spirit, to grow ever closer to God. In the highest degree of love of God, the soul loses consciousness of itself, becomes nothing and is absorbed into God (union with God). To be touched by this love is to become like God.' Most of us have still some way to go.

Jesus Christ, God the Son, the second member of the Trinity, taught about the Father's will and revealed the Holy Spirit. We dwell on Him in the next chapter.

Chapter 7

JESUS CHRIST, SON OF GOD

My early childhood concept of Jesus was that He was gentle and full of love and I was taught that He was the Son of God. At the time it never occurred to me to question His divinity and nothing I have heard or read since has given me the slightest cause to do so. There is something called faith, which is fundamental to our relationship with God. Jesus Himself emphasised the importance of faith many times, particularly with regard to healing and to prayer. For example: 'Whatever you ask for in prayer, believe that you have received it and it will be yours' (Mark 11:24). Fundamental to Christian faith must be belief in Jesus Christ as Lord, the Son of God, born of the Virgin Mary. These days there are many who think they are cleverer than the holy Scriptures and who question the credentials of Christ Jesus. I regard this as something far worse than arrogance.

Although I have never questioned the divinity of Jesus that I was taught in infancy, I have learned that He was much more than the 'gentle Jesus meek and mild' image of my initiation. My favourite author, Nevil Shute, always prized the qualities of tenderness and courage. They shine out in his novels with a steady light. I corresponded with Nevil Shute and we planned to meet but, sadly, he died in Australia before his next visit to England. His daughter visited us and told me that the book he was working on at the time of his death did have a Christian connection. I am sure that most people have had friends whose tenderness and courage shine out. Sadly, but predictably, three outstanding examples who were friends of mine were killed in the Second World War.

No one could aspire to the depths of compassion, love and tenderness of Jesus. In compassion He raised both Lazarus and the son of the widow of Nain from the dead. In compassion He healed the sick and exorcised evil spirits. Jesus was seen to weep and on a number of occasions He emphasised His love of children and their importance.

> Unless you turn round and become like children, you will never enter the kingdom of Heaven. Whoever humbles himself and becomes like this child will be the greatest in the kingdom of Heaven, and whoever receives one such child in my name receives me. But if anyone causes the downfall of one of these little ones who believe in me, it would be better for him to have a millstone hung round his neck and be drowned in the depths of the sea.
>
> (Matthew 18:3–6)

As a lover of children, our Lord must have been deeply touched, as we were in 1999, by this gesture by a child. Lorraine, a lovely thirty-five-year-old wife and mother, tragically died during a very serious operation. A day or so later, when her five-year-old daughter Emily was given a box of chocolates, she said: 'I will take them to Jesus and ask Him to give them to mummy.'

Yes, He was full of love and tenderness, yet no one could emulate the physical and moral courage of Jesus, defying the highest authority of the high priests and the rulers; not secretly undermining them, but tackling them head on; not mincing His words but boldly denouncing them. He showed up their hypocrisy, ridiculing the smallness of their minds. The scribes and Pharisees bore the full weight of his invective; their hypocrisy drove Him to denunciation in the strongest terms and the invective contained in Matthew 23:1–33 eclipses anything that a politician could say in Parliament against the Opposition:

Jesus then addressed the crowds and his disciples in these words: 'The scribes and the Pharisees occupy Moses' seat; so be careful to do whatever they tell you. But do not follow their practice; for they say one thing and do another. They make up heavy loads and pile them on the shoulders of others, but will not themselves lift a finger to ease the burden. Whatever they do is done for show . . . they love to have the place of honour at feasts and the chief seats in synagogues.

. . . Alas for you, scribes and Pharisees, hypocrites! You shut the door of the kingdom of Heaven in people's faces; you do not enter yourselves, and when others try to enter, you stop them. Alas for you, scribes and Pharisees, hypocrites! You travel over sea and land to win one convert; and when you have succeeded you make him twice as fit for hell as you are yourselves . . . Blind fools! . . . you have over-looked the weightier demands of the law – justice, mercy, and good faith. It is these you should have practised, without neglecting the others. Blind guides! You strain off a midge, yet gulp down a camel!

Alas for you, scribes and Pharisees, hypocrites! You clean the outside of a cup or a dish, and leave the inside full of greed and self-indulgence! . . . You are like tombs covered with whitewash; they look fine on the outside, but inside they are full of dead men's bones and of corruption. So it is with you: outwardly you look like honest men, but inside you are full of hypocrisy and lawlessness . . . So you acknowledge that you are the sons of those who killed the Prophets. Go on then, finish off what your fathers began! Snakes! Vipers' brood! How can you escape being condemned to hell?'

Jesus would never shrink from stating what He knew to be right or from condemning what He knew to be wrong. Unlike a politician, He would not say what He hoped would gain Him popularity. Increasingly it was apparent that the authorities would find a means of doing away with Him. Jesus knew full well the agony of the horrendous slow death by crucifixion and in the Garden of Gethsemane He prayed that the cup might pass from Him: 'Yet not my will but thine be done.'

Few people dispute the fact of the trial and crucifixion of Jesus. Even those who do not accept His divinity acknowledge His exceptional powers and His integrity and courage. Of course, if someone is the Son of God one should not be concerned about their personal qualities, but if they are, like Jesus, utterly admirable and without stain it does help!

Until the age of thirty Jesus appears to have led a normal life, working as a carpenter with Joseph at Nazareth. Mary and Joseph were aware of the divinity of Jesus and He himself indicated His awareness at the age of twelve, when He went missing and was found in the temple discussing with the rabbis (Luke 2:43–50). John the Baptist was sent to proclaim His coming (Mark 1:7). The ministry of Jesus lasted less than four years, commencing at His baptism by John in the River Jordan. After the baptism, Jesus went straight out into the wilderness in solitude, prayer and fasting for forty days, during which time He was tempted by the devil. Fasting is no longer common among church people during Lent but occasional fasting or just giving up things we enjoy, such as alcohol or chocolate, is a small discipline, a token offering to God, which helps to remind us of our Lord's forty days in the wilderness. Most of us would also benefit from spending more time in prayer 'in the wilderness'.

Our Lord's ministry consisted of teaching, healing and speaking out against things that were wrong. He spent a great deal of time in prayer and contemplation. Building up the apostolate and training them was a priority: choosing men who would become dedicated believers and who were capable of continuing His ministry. They would need to be men of fibre, prepared to suffer taunts, persecution, imprisonment and martyrdom. It is significant that Jesus Himself spent considerable time in prayer over their selection.

The apostles were a mixed bunch of outstanding and dedicated men, and included fishermen, a tax collector and a physician. After His death, resurrection and ascension, Jesus converted Saul, renamed Paul, the arch-enemy of the Christians, and used him to great effect (Acts 9:1–30). St John, to whom Jesus, at His crucifixion, had entrusted Mary, His mother, lived to a great age in exile, mainly at Ephesus and Patmos, where he wrote the book of Revelation.

Teaching, preaching and healing were linked. People were attentive to the teaching, often in parables, but it was the miracles of healing that really impressed and made people realise that Jesus was someone very special, perhaps the Messiah. They had to take His teaching seriously. Paul eventually saw Jesus as someone 'in whom all the treasures of wisdom and knowledge are hidden'.

Jesus was very practical, as well as being spiritual. If His teaching and the Father's commandments had been followed it would have become a near perfect world – and would be so today. 'I have come that they might have life, and may have it in all its fullness' (John 10:10). Our Lord commended the humble and meek. Certainly they will find faith before the clever ones who quibble and question miracles such as the Virgin birth, unable to accept anything which their minds cannot understand or the reality of the love and power of God.

Jesus, of course, was more aware than anyone that man is both material body and spirit. He taught how we should live our lives in accordance with the will of God. Many times He emphasised the greater importance of the spiritual and of putting our trust in God. For example, in one of the most beautiful passages in the New Testament: 'Consider the lilies of the field, how they grow; they toil not, neither do they spin: And yet I say unto you, that even Solomon in all his glory was not arrayed like one of these . . . if God so clothe the grass of the field, which to day is, and to morrow is cast into the oven, shall he not much more clothe you, O ye of little faith?' (Matthew 6:28–30 AV).

The Pharisees, always trying to trap Jesus, asked Him whether it was lawful to give tribute to Caesar. They received the answer: 'Render therefore unto Caesar the things that are Caesar's; and unto God the things that are God's.' In our times, and almost certainly in every age, 'Caesar' has more than received his due and God has been short-changed. Not only was He good, loving, compassionate, tender yet full of courage and strong, He was also wise. Realistic too and aware of the way of the world. He had been sent to live with men and women on earth and He knew the problems, the pitfalls and the temptations. He understood our earthly existence, but more important than that He understood the relationship between the earthly existence and the Heavenly Kingdom, eternal life. He knew and taught how we could serve the Father amidst our daily earthly life, loving Him, serving Him, obeying Him. It is all contained very simply and clearly in the teachings of Jesus and He lived it out in His own life, not least in the time He spent in prayer. He made very clear in His teaching that love must be at the centre, our love of God and our love of one another, not sentimental love but love in a practical form, treating people as if we love them. What a difference it would make if we could all practice that today!

It is worth spending time in contemplation of the teaching of Jesus. I was not particularly keen on Scripture at school, but the older I get the more I realise the practical importance of our Lord's teaching and its relevance to our lives today. How we still reject Him! So what was this teaching? Most important was instruction on relationships, how we treat one another, particularly love and forgiveness. Jesus had much to say on the subject:

- In answer to the question: 'Which is the first of all the commandments?' (Mark 12:28) 'He answered: ". . . love the Lord your God with all your heart, with all your soul, with all your mind, and with all your strength." The second is this: "You must love your neighbour as yourself."'
- 'Always treat others as you would like them to treat you: that is the law and the prophets' (Matthew 7:12). Many of us were brought up on: 'Do as you would be done by,' and had not realised its source!
- 'I am the good shepherd . . . and I lay down my life for the sheep' (John 10:14–15).
- 'Do not judge, and you will not be judged' (Matthew 7:1).
- 'First take the plank out of your own eye, and then you will see clearly to take the speck out of your brother's' (Matthew 7:5).
- '. . . whoever hears these words of mine and acts on them is like a man who had the sense to build his house on rock' (Matthew 7:24).

In the course of the Sermon on the Mount our Lord emphasised the goodness of the meek, the righteous, the merciful, the pure, the peacemakers and the persecuted. Reconciliation and forgiveness featured strongly in His teaching: not 'an eye for an eye, a tooth for a tooth' but 'turn the other cheek' – in our day a lesson that many, including the Jews, still do not accept. 'Love your enemies; do good to those who hate you; bless those who curse you' (Luke 6:27–28). It is easy to dismiss such teaching as impractical and certainly it is not easy to apply, but it is likely to lead to a happier outcome than festering hatred. If you love only those who love you, what reward can you expect? Even the tax collectors do as much as that. If you greet only your brothers, what is so extraordinary about that? Even the heathen do as much.

'There must be no limit to your goodness, as your Heavenly Father's goodness knows no bounds.' Jesus pointed people to Heaven, the Father's Kingdom. 'Do not store up for yourselves treasure on earth . . . but store up treasure in Heaven, where neither moth nor rust will destroy, nor thieves break in and steal. For where your treasure is, there will your heart be also' (Matthew 6:19–21). How relevant that is in our affluent society today!

Jesus was not interested in popularity and many of His teachings, such as 'love your enemies', were unlikely to find favour, practical though they were. Resentment and bitterness can become festering poisons and so many families suffer from these quite unnecessarily. Sometimes the cause of resentment is a complete misunderstanding. If there is a feeling of bitterness or resentment the remedy is to be open, to discuss, resolve and forgive. To fail to be reconciled is not only to cause continuing bitterness, often at a deeper level, but is also disobedience to the teaching of Jesus and to the will of God. He wants us to live sound, satisfying lives and tells us how to do so:

- Matthew 5:23–25 – 'So if you are presenting your gift at

the altar and suddenly remember that your brother has a grievance against you, leave your gift where it is before the altar. First go and make peace with your brother; then come back and offer your gift. If someone sues you, come to terms with him promptly.'

- Matthew 5:33–37 – 'You have heard that our forefathers were told: ". . . Oaths sworn to the Lord must be kept." But what I tell you is this: You are not to swear at all . . . Plain "Yes" or "No" is all you need to say.'

- Matthew 5:38 – 'You have heard that they were told, "An eye for an eye, a tooth for a tooth." But what I tell you is this: Do not resist those who wrong you. If anyone slaps you on the right cheek, turn and offer him the other also.'

Most of us would find this difficult, but Jesus himself complied, putting up no resistance when He was arrested, flogged and crucified. Peter, at the time of the arrest in the Garden of Gethsemane, was rebuked by Jesus and told to put away his sword when he had cut off the ear of the High Priest's servant. Jesus then healed the ear.

I am increasingly aware of the significance of love. Love is at the centre of all Jesus' teaching. Love and forgiveness. Love God, love your neighbour, love your enemies. Equally important is the fact that God loves and forgives us. The day when anyone becomes aware of the reality of God's love for them their life changes. Countless people have discovered this but it is something that I would not have realised had it not happened to me. Such things are not given for personal satisfaction but to be made known to others and used to God's glory.

In our world today we are accustomed to rapid change. Even fifty years ago life was very different. Man had not been in space, computers were vast machines built for special projects and used only by research organisations and large companies, mobile phones were unknown, the Channel Tunnel had not been constructed and Britain had no motorways. So much change in only fifty years, yet although a few of the teachings of Jesus, nearly two thousand years ago, appear somewhat extreme in our permissive age, they are as relevant and significant today as they were to the people of His time. Our Lord's teachings on wealth are well known. 'It is easier for a camel to pass through the eye of a needle than for a rich man to enter the Kingdom of God' (Matthew 19:24). To the rich young man He said: 'One thing you lack . . . Go, sell everything you have, and give to the poor.' The man went away sorrowing.

If Christ's teachings were followed, it would be a near-perfect world, with no real poverty, no wars and fewer broken homes. Many do try to keep the commandments and follow at least most of the teachings of Jesus. Our Lord set down in the parable of the sower (Matthew 13:3–9, 19–23), reasons why people fall away from God and do not try to follow His teaching. The seed that falls among thorns or thistles represents those who hear the word but worldly cares and the false glamour of wealth choke it. Surely that is as applicable today as it was two thousand years ago. Shortly after writing this, I heard a BBC News item about a poor country in South America. It was said that the people were so poor that they had no possessions but they cared much more about one another than we in the West, who are too concerned about our wealth and possessions to show concern for our neighbours.

Although very aware of the effects of wealth and materialism on the spiritual life I had not previously given thought to the equally devastating effect on social values. 'A thief comes only to steal, kill, and destroy; I have come that they may have life and have it in all its fullness. I am the good shepherd; the good shepherd lays down his life for the sheep' (John 10:10). The parable of the prodigal son (Luke

15:11–31) emphasises God's forgiveness for those who
return to Him after turning away to sin. Likewise, the
parable of the lost sheep demonstrates God's joy over one
sinner who repents (Matthew 18:12). The parable of the
sheep and the goats (Matthew 25:32–46) is one to which we
all need to respond. It is every bit as relevant to us today as
when first spoken by Jesus:

> Then the king will say to those on his right, 'You have
> my Father's blessing; come, take possession of the
> Kingdom that has been ready for you since the world
> was made. For when I was hungry, you gave me food;
> when thirsty, you gave me drink; when I was a stranger,
> you took me into your home; when naked, you clothed
> me; when I was ill, you came to my help; when in
> prison, you visited me.' Then the righteous will reply,
> 'Lord, when . . . did we see you ill or in prison . . . ?'
> And the king will answer, '. . . anything you did for one
> of my brothers here, however insignificant, you did for
> me.'

Nothing could be clearer than that. And if we do these
things, knowing that we are acting in the will of God (but
not for reward) they become no longer a burden but a
privilege. But for those who are unimpressed, consider verses
41–46 – 'Then he will say to those on his left, ". . . go from
my sight to the eternal fire . . . For when I was hungry, you
gave me nothing to eat; when thirsty, nothing to drink . . .
when I was ill and in prison, you did not come to my help."'
Yes, we can all make excuses, but every time I read these
passages I resolve to do better. I have taken just a few of our
Lord's teachings. There are many more and every one is
relevant to us today. We have the benefit of the Scriptures
for our guidance and may we try harder to live in accordance
with God's will.

'No one comes to the Father except by me' (John 14:6). I suspect that this uncompromising verse causes more problems than any other in the Gospels. We have seen that although Jesus was gentle and sensitive, He was also bold and forthright and nothing He said was designed to curry favour. This statement was part of our Lord's farewell talk to the apostles and needs to be taken in context. Chapter 14 commences:

'Set your troubled hearts at rest . . . I am going to prepare a place for you. And if I go and prepare a place for you, I shall come again and take you to myself, so that where I am you may be also; and you know the way I am taking.' Thomas said, 'Lord, we do not know where you are going, so how can we know the way?' Jesus replied, 'I am the way, the truth, and the life; no one comes to the Father except by me.'

It is, of course, a fact that no one does come to the Father except by following the Son. We cannot go direct to the Father, but by acknowledging and worshipping the Son, who redeemed us and acknowledged the supremacy of His Father. For me there is also great significance in our Lord's words to the disciples: 'As the Father sent me, so send I you' (John 20:21).

These days, there are so many who no longer believe in Almighty God. There is increasing interest in the occult, as well as worship of the idols of wealth and materialism, and there are now many people of other faiths. It seems right that there should be complete freedom for other religions to worship God in their own way. Personally I am happy to have friends who are Jews, Muslims and Buddhists but I am one hundred percent Christian and accept the word of Jesus that my way to Heaven is only through Him. I am grateful for that clear and uncompromising message on how to get there. Spoken in the knowledge that He was about to display His own love in terrible agony on the cross, the final instruction of Jesus to His disciples was: 'Love one another as I have loved you.' Perhaps the most encouraging words our Lord ever spoke were among His last from the cross, to one of the criminals crucified with Him: 'Today you will be with me in Paradise' (Luke 23:43).

Paintings of Jesus abound but there are, of course, no contemporary portraits or photographs to show us what He looked like. Our friend and colleague, the Reverend Pat Ashe, has an original picture of Jesus, painted in 1928 in response to a vision. Helen Brookfield King, sitting alone one afternoon, suddenly saw this wonderful face. As the artist recorded: 'Once, the most beautiful head of a man came to me in a vision. I painted it, and many people say it was my best portrait.' The figure stood before he, in a vision, for a full ten minutes and the vividness of the vision and the divine power and sensitivity in the expression made her realise it could only be Jesus Christ and she exclaimed out loud: 'Oh, that is what He looked like!' She felt it was an answer to a prayer, often made, that she should one day be shown what Christ looked like when on earth. Some people are concerned at the short hair and no beard. However a rabbi, whose learning had won him the honour of a knighthood, on seeing the picture said that these details were absolutely correct, as young Jews of Christ's day did not wear the hair long, and often had moustaches without beards. The robe of golden brown with the tassel attached was also, said the rabbi, quite correct. You may like to take a good look at the picture and then re-read, say, pages 93, 94.

Of course, we do not need pictures of Jesus in order to know Him, for now through His Spirit He lives in us and we in Him. Yet this is an important picture. It was given through a vision, yet another gift from God. There is tremen-dous strength in that figure, yet deep sensitivity in the eyes. Here is someone who would stand up and confront authority, who one can imagine overturning the tables of the money changers in His Father's House saying 'You have made it a den of theves.' Yet one can also hear him saying 'let the little children come to me'.

I have narrated in Chapter 4 how I became involved with the unveiling of the mystical picture of Jesus, 'The Living Christ'. The artist believed that the picture was to bring awareness to the sick and suffering of Christ's compassion for them. I am certain that there is a further message for all people. There is a terrible sadness, particularly in the eyes . . . real hurt. This is more than compassion; it is also the hurt of continuing rejection. In the right hand is a small cross, a reminder of His great suffering and sacrifice undertaken for us. As He looks down upon the world what does He see? – His teaching ignored, the Father's commandments broken, the resulting wars, violence, hatred, broken homes. Excess affluence and arrogance contrasting with the desperate poverty, hunger and suffering of millions who receive no help. The picture echoes the words of Our Lady at Fatima in 1917: 'Do not offend Our Lord any more. He is already offended too much.'

Jesus came and taught and died so that the world might be redeemed. I believe that He did inspire this picture in order to plead with us to remember His teaching and that it was for us that He died that agonising death on the cross so that we might inherit eternal life. It is not too late for any of us to respond.

Chapter 8

THE CHRISTIAN HEALING MINISTRY: FROM THE BEGINNING

Jesus was full of compassion, which is one reason why His healing ministry occupies no less than twenty-five per cent of the New Testament Gospels. Jesus healed people who were sick, lame, blind, deaf and dumb and those suffering from leprosy. He cast out devils and He raised from the dead Lazarus, the son of the widow of Nain and the daughter of Jairus. On the first two of these occasions it is clear that compassion was our Lord's motivation. In the case of Lazarus He was deeply moved by the weeping sisters Martha and Mary. The widow of Nain was very poor and the son who died had provided her only source of income. The apostles and others were with Jesus when he carried out miracles of healing. They learned from Him and He gave them authority over unclean spirits and to cure every illness (Matthew 10:1).

I was over fifty when I first discovered that the Christian healing ministry was active in our own times. Most people know of our Lord's miracles of healing, continued after the ascension by the disciples and Paul, and recorded in the book of Acts. But in our days? Many people are still unaware of the great expansion which has taken place in the Christian healing ministry in the past thirty years, not only here but in the USA, Africa and throughout the world.

I was the guest of a Nigerian chief, a Muslim, when the seventeen-year-old barefoot local girl who was tidying my room saw my Bible and asked if she could read from it. The passage happened to be one of our Lord's miracles of healing. 'Healing miracles are happening today, Alice,' I commented. 'Oh yes, I know, we have healing services in our church every Thursday evening' she replied! On arrival in another country, I mentioned to my Muslim host that in the Christian Church we had a healing ministry and asked if they had anything similar in the Muslim religion. I was stunned by the reply: 'We have some sick people coming to our house for ministry this evening.' Two American Christian missionary ladies appeared and had supper with us and I had the privilege of joining them in laying hands on these people, our hosts not being present.

So, what is the Christian healing ministry? One well-known person responded to me: 'It's when you touch someone on the shoulder and say a phrase, isn't it?' Well, you could say that but I prefer Bishop Morris Maddocks': 'The Christian Healing Ministry is bringing Jesus Christ to the point of your need.' How do we minister God's healing? Fundamentally it is very simple. We follow the teaching and example of Jesus Christ and His disciples. However, there are many aspects of Christian healing and hundreds of books have been written on the subject in the last twenty years. Soon after I first became aware of this ministry I went on a retreat on the subject under the Reverend Dr Martin Israel, a revered mystic, priest and lecturer to the Royal College of Surgeons. He commenced the three-day retreat by saying: 'Christian healing is about being open to God and open to our fellow beings in need.' This was, I believe, as near as he got to telling us how to minister healing.

Martin Israel is a man of deep faith and wisdom. It must be the first essential to open ourselves to God, for we are merely His channels for healing and a channel must be open to be effective. Dorothy Kerin put it: 'We are just pieces of pipe.' We must also be open to the person to be healed so that we can know what needs to be healed. It may well be that there is something deeper causing the illness or pain and this must first be removed before healing can take place. Among the most common barriers are sin and guilt, fear and worry. Until these have been got rid of, through 'inner healing', healing of the illness or other problem cannot take place. Jesus, of course, was aware of this. When the paralysed man was let down through the roof for healing He immediately said: 'Your sins are forgiven'. Later He also healed the paralysis. I must not give the impression that Christian healing is complicated, because fundamentally it is very simple and many people have been healed through the prayers of children. There is, however, a great deal that can be learned about the ministry and a few of the hundreds of books available are mentioned in Appendix 3.

We cannot be completely healthy unless we are whole in body, mind and spirit, and only through God can we be made whole in spirit. Prayers for healing are not always answered in the way we expect. Miracles do indeed happen every day and we believe that prayer is always answered, but it is presumptuous to believe that God will always answer our prayer in the way we want or expect. We pray in faith asking for what we believe to be right but leaving the answer in His hands. 'Thy will be done.'

In this ministry we are continuing the work of our Lord and His apostles, Paul and the disciples, so it seems appropriate to remind ourselves of their ministry and to ensure that we follow the teaching and example that we are set. Preaching the Kingdom of God and healing were to be combined and our Lord emphasised that through these miracles glory must be given to the Father. Jesus healed people who were sick, lame, blind, deaf and dumb as well as lepers. He cast out devils and, on three recorded occasions, He raised from the dead – Lazarus, the son of the widow of Nain, and the daughter of Jairus. On the first two occasions it is clear that compassion was our Lord's motivation, in the case of Lazarus, He was deeply moved by the weeping sisters Martha and Mary. The widow of Nain was very poor and the son had provided her only source of income.

The apostles and others were with Jesus when He carried out the miracles of healing and He taught them. Jesus called his twelve apostles to Him and gave them authority to drive out unclean spirits and to cure every kind of illness and infirmity. 'I send you out like sheep among wolves; be wary as serpents, innocent as doves' (Matthew 10:16). Sometime later Jesus selected a further seventy-two men and sent them out in pairs (Luke 10:1). He gave them authority:

'Whoever listens to you listens to me; whoever rejects you rejects me. And whoever rejects me rejects the One who sent me.' The seventy-two came back jubilant. 'In your name, Lord,' they said, 'even the demons submit to us.' He replied: 'I saw Satan fall, like lightning, from Heaven.'

One can imagine the jubilation of the disciples over the success of their mission and I suspect that our Lord would have had a twinkle in His eye as He made that remark about Satan. Perhaps those of us involved in this ministry should evidence more enthusiasm and joy when we witness the power of God triumphant. It might help to kill the myth that 'religion is boring'!

Largely as a result of the miracles of healing performed by Jesus, His fame and reputation spread and people flocked to Him wherever He went. Many times He had to climb to a secluded spot or get into a boat to escape them in order to have time for peace and prayer. We, in our day, also need to make time for peace and quiet to be alone with God and to receive His discernment.

'Preach the Kingdom of God and heal the sick.' This was

our Lord's command to His followers and it continued to be obeyed, after His ascension, by the apostles and disciples. The result was that people believed the teaching because they experienced the power of God through witnessing the healings. In Matthew 10:7 it is recorded that the apostles were sent out with the instruction to 'proclaim the message: "The kingdom of Heaven is upon you." Heal the sick, raise the dead, cleanse lepers, drive out demons. You have received without cost; give without charge.' Did this instruction apply just in our Lord's day or does He really mean us to continue to heal in God's name today? I am utterly certain that He does. During His short period on earth, after the resurrection, our Lord empowered the disciples to continue His ministry throughout the world: 'As my Father sent me, even so send I you.' There could be no greater authorisation than that.

After the ascension, one of the great opponents of Christianity, a man named Saul, was on a journey to Damascus to persecute Christians. Saul had a terrifying experience, which completely changed his life. He was suddenly thrown to the ground by an unseen power and blinded. '"Tell me, Lord," he said, "who you are." The voice answered, "I am Jesus, whom you are persecuting."' (Acts 9:5). Three days later the Lord sent Ananias to lay hands on Saul, who was immediately healed of the blindness and was baptised. Saul, renamed Paul, joined the disciples in preaching, teaching and healing. Paul's main ministry was concerned with boldly proclaiming the Kingdom of God. He had a well-educated background and was so bold and passionate in his love of the Lord that one would have expected that the preaching and teaching role in a hostile environment would have suited him more than the compassionate role of healing. Yet we read in Acts 19:11–12 that 'God worked extraordinary miracles through Paul: when handkerchiefs and scarves which had been in contact with his skin were carried to the sick, they were cured of their diseases, and the evil spirits came out of them.' This is amazing, bearing in mind that Paul had not worked with Jesus and was a relative newcomer to the ministry, .

In Acts 13:8 we read that Elymas the magician approached Paul and Barnabas when they were preaching to a high official. Paul, filled with the Holy Spirit, says to Elymas: 'You are a swindler, an out-and-out fraud! You son of the devil and enemy of all goodness . . . the hand of the Lord strikes: you shall be blind, and for a time you shall not see the light of the sun.' Elymas went blind but 'When the governor saw what had happened he became a believer, deeply impressed by what he learnt about the Lord.' It was the blinding that demonstrated the power but the teaching that brought the belief. It is significant that Paul is reported as 'filled with the Holy Spirit'. It is in the power of the Holy Spirit that miracles are worked and anyone healing in the name of the Lord needs to be prayerfully open to the Holy Spirit.

Acts 8:5–8 records that Philip went to a city in Samaria and proclaimed the Messiah to them. 'As the crowds heard Philip and saw the signs he performed, everyone paid close attention to what he had to say . . . many paralysed and crippled folk were cured; and there was great rejoicing in that city'.

Acts 3:2–16 is a very significant passage, an example on how to combine the ministry of Christian healing with evangelism, either in the days of the disciples or now. At the temple gate, Peter and John heal a beggar who had been a cripple from birth:

Peter said, 'I have no silver or gold; but what I have I give you: in the name of Jesus Christ of Nazareth, get up and walk.' . . . he sprang to his feet, and . . . entered the temple with them, leaping and praising God.' . . .

when they recognised him they were filled with wonder and amazement . . . Peter . . . met them with these words: 'Men of Israel, why be surprised at this? Why stare at us as if we had made this man walk by some power or godliness of our own? . . . God raised him from the dead; of that we are witnesses. The name of Jesus, by awakening faith, has given strength to this man whom you see and know, and this faith has made him completely well as you can all see . . . Repent, therefore, and turn to God, so that your sins may be wiped out.'

Before Peter and John completed their address to the people, they were arrested and put in prison for the night. 'But many of those who had heard the message became believers, bringing the number of men to about five thousand' (Acts 4:4). We could not have a better example of how to give glory to God for the healing and combine this with exhortation to repent and turn to God. Understandably, it brought a rich harvest of new believers. This is badly needed today, when there are thousands of so-called 'healers' who take both glory for themselves and financial reward. Under interrogation by the court, Peter,

. . . filled with the Holy Spirit, answered, 'Rulers of the people and elders, if it is about help given to a sick man that we are being questioned today, and the means by which he was cured, this is our answer to all of you and to all the people of Israel: it was by the name of Jesus Christ of Nazareth, whom you crucified, and whom God raised from the dead; through him this man stands here before you fit and well.'

In order to stop the news of the miracle spreading further Peter and John were ordered to refrain from all public speaking and teaching in the name of Jesus. 'But Peter and John replied: "Is it right in the eyes of God for us to obey you rather than him? Judge for yourselves. We cannot possibly give up speaking about what we have seen and heard."' Peter and John returned to their friends and reported what had happened. They prayed together:

'. . . enable those who serve you to speak your word with all boldness. Stretch out your hand to heal and cause signs and portents to be done through the name of your holy servant Jesus.' When they had ended their prayer, the building where they were assembled rocked, and all were filled with the Holy Spirit and spoke God's word with boldness.

The above prayer is now adapted as the Acorn Christian Healing Trust prayer.

This passage is a copybook example of 'how to do it'. Not only, as noted above, for giving glory to God and combining it with the invitation to repentance but in following our Lord's instruction that the apostles should not worry about how to answer their accusers, but that the Holy Spirit would give them utterance. Peter would not have been 'filled with the Holy Spirit' if he had been worrying about how to respond and trying to work out his defence. We too need to remember to open ourselves to the Holy Spirit when we have to speak out for the Lord or when we need guidance or power for healing. These events happened nearly two thousand years ago but they are just as relevant to us today. At times, healings brought unexpected problems, as in Acts 14:8:

At Lystra a cripple, lame from birth, who had never walked in his life, sat listening to Paul as he spoke. Paul fixed his eyes on him and, seeing that he had the faith to be cured, said in a loud voice, 'Stand up straight on your feet'; and he sprang up and began to walk. When the crowds saw what Paul had done, they shouted, in their native Lycaonian, 'The gods have come down to us in human form!' They called Barnabas Zeus and Paul they called Hermes, because he was the spokesman. The priest of Zeus, whose temple was just outside the city, brought oxen and garlands to the gates, and he and the people were about to offer sacrifice. But when the apostles Barnabas and Paul heard of it, they tore their clothes and rushed into the crowd shouting, 'Men, why are you doing this? We are human beings, just like you. The good news we bring tells you to turn from these follies to the living God, who made Heaven and earth and sea and everything in them' . . . Even with these words they barely managed to prevent the crowd from offering sacrifice to them.

You may think that is one problem unlikely to be faced by our ministry of healing. But the Reverend Russ Parker, Director of Acorn Healing Trust, tells of his alarming experience at a conference in 1988 at Pescara, Italy. He does not speak Italian and few of the delegates had any knowledge of English. Apparently, one of Russ's books on Christian healing had, without permission, been published in Italian. During a coffee break people went up to Russ to get him to sign their copies. They asked him to bless them and he made the sign of the cross on each forehead and prayed a simple prayer of blessing in English. He had no idea of their individual needs and they had no idea of what he was praying. A number were overcome by the power of the Holy Spirit and fell to the floor and others began to run around the room and shout praises to God. The interpreter informed Russ that these people were reporting that they were being healed. They included a lady who had been lame for many years. Immediately the queue became a mass of over one hundred people wanting laying on of hands. More healings were reported and Russ was overdue for the next speaking session. He was then provided with two 'minders' who fended off the queue of people anxious to be prayed for, some throwing themselves down in front of him to touch his feet in the hope of a healing. The next two days he went about everywhere with two 'minders', he had to eat on his own and the lift had to be guarded so that he would not be bothered when going up to his room. Russ had no time for himself, there were constant requests for prayer and a touch of God seemed to immediately follow each prayer. Russ was thrilled to see the healings but understandably became uncomfortable with the consequences.

We can understand why Jesus exhorted some of his patients to keep quiet about their healings, but they told everyone, with the result that He could not continue His work among them but had to leave the district. Russ experienced a different problem. People hearing of such healings expect them to continue, but with Russ it did not continue beyond the conference and, of course, people were disappointed and upset. Undoubtedly, the most important lesson from this is the reminder that the flow of the power of God through the Holy Spirit is enabled by faith and expectancy.

In Acts 9:36 it is revealed that the apostle Peter raised from the dead a disciple, Tabitha. 'Peter sent them all outside, and knelt down and prayed; then, turning towards the body, he said: "Tabitha, get up." She opened her eyes, saw Peter and sat up . . . News of it spread all over Joppa, and many came to believe in the Lord.' In Acts 9:32 'Peter . . . went down to visit God's people at Lydda. There he found a man named Aeneas who had been bedridden with paralysis for eight years. Peter said to him, "Aeneas, Jesus Christ cures you; get up and make your bed!" and immediately he stood up. All who lived in Lydda and Sharon saw him; and they turned to the Lord.'

Paul and the other apostles faithfully carried out our Lord's instructions to preach, teach and heal in His name. Because they were obedient and prayerful, they were filled with zeal and with the Holy Spirit. As a result of this preaching and healing, in a largely hostile environment, thousands were converted to Christ and churches were established over a wide area. What an example for us! What can we learn about what we should be doing in the Christian healing ministry? Teaching and healing in the power of the Holy Spirit, through Jesus Christ our Lord and in His name. This applies to every Christian denomination throughout the world, yet I was not even aware that there was still a Christian healing ministry until I was fifty-five years old!

We are to 'proclaim the kingdom of Heaven' in conjunction with our healing ministry. I would interpret this as evangelising in our own way, emphasising the gifts given by God, including peace. Always we must lay on hands and pray in the name of Jesus, or of the Father, Son and Holy Spirit. This is absolutely essential today: Give God the glory. Believe. Faith plays a big part, not only the faith of the person ministering, but that of the patient also. Remember the woman who touched His garment and was healed of her issue of blood. The importance of the Holy Spirit is shown again and again in Acts and this entails time for prayer and preparation. Boldness also is mentioned and although, happily, we in this country do not risk physical opposition, we have friends ministering in a country where they and their converts are in daily peril of punishment and possible death. Even we sometimes need moral courage to mention the Lord's healing in public. I am not one to ask people if they are 'saved' but talking about the Christian healing ministry is different and acceptable and I make a point of trying to get in a word about it in conversation at social functions. This has produced quite interesting results. Members of the medical profession tend to be disinterested while top marks go to a member of the royal family. The importance of the testimony of people who have received God's healing was shown in the time of Jesus and of Acts and so it is today. We have produced a video, *Steps of Faith*, which includes remarkable testimonies of healing from three of our associates. Another includes testimonies from members of our Christian Cancer Help Centre. The rule of the Christian healing ministry, that no charge is made, is in obedience to our Lord's instruction to the disciples not to accept any reward: 'You have received without cost, give without charge.'

As we have noted, the disciples obeyed our Lord's instruction to continue the work of healing and preaching. They did so diligently, in accordance with His teaching and example. Many of us today feel called into this ministry. It is an awesome privilege and responsibility.

Jesus was constantly praying to the Father. If it was necessary for Jesus to pray, it is all the more important that we should pray that we might be guided and directed by the Holy Spirit. The closer we are to Jesus, the better we can serve Him, ministering in His name. Power and discernment are essential for the healing ministry and these are among the fruits of prayer.

It is recorded of Jesus in Luke 5:17 that: '. . . the power of the Lord was with him to heal the sick.' This immediately precedes the healing of the paralysed man let down through the roof. If Jesus needed God's power, all the more do we need it and it is still available if we are called to serve as His channels. In John 5:19 we read: '. . . the Son can do nothing by himself . . . whatever the Father does, the Son does . . . As the Father raises the dead and gives them life, so the Son gives life as he chooses.' Our Lord was direct and straightforward, sensitive to the needs of individuals and often driven by compassion. No healing services as such are recorded. As news of the miracles spread people flocked to Him. Everyone receiving ministry from our Lord was healed, though a blind man initially was only partially healed, then after further ministry the healing was completed (Mark 8:23–25). It is worth noting that at the Pool of Siloam, only one person was healed, the cripple who had been unable to reach the water in time, due to his infirmities. The other sick people were left to find their healing at the pool (John 5:3–8).

There is at least one case of distant healing recorded, in Luke 7:3–10. The centurion whose servant was dying says: 'Do not trouble further, sir; I am not worthy to have you come under my roof . . . But say the word and my servant will be cured. I know, for I am myself under orders, with soldiers under me. I say to one: "Go," and he goes; to another, "Come here," and he comes . . .' When Jesus heard this he said: 'I tell you, not even in Israel have I found such faith.' The servant was healed, through the faith of his master. The centurion knew that the power of Jesus could heal without His being present in person. This is a very significant passage because that is the position we are in today. Jesus is not here in person, but His Spirit is available to us if we call upon Him in openness and faith.

The faith and expectancy of the patient is very significant in healing. Yet we must never say: 'It is your fault that you are not healed, you lack sufficient faith.' Only God can know or say that. We are merely His servants. We need to be open to God so that we may receive His guidance and His power. We are the channels through which God heals today. Follow as closely as possible the example of Jesus and keep it simple. The closer we come to Him the better we can serve.

So many people do not take these miraculous healings seriously. Why? It all happened so long ago. If they are ill, they go to their doctor. They regard anyone who seriously believes in miraculous healing today as suffering from religious mania. But let us examine the evidence.

The Christian Church was established and grew quite rapidly throughout the world. There have been saints, martyrs and miracles all down the centuries. Unfortunately, the healing ministry got neglected and only became rekindled during the last century. In the past fifty years or so there has been rapid growth throughout the world. It is unreasonable and illogical to believe that the Christian Church could have expanded so rapidly throughout the world if there had been no miraculous powers in evidence. St Paul had been a strict Jew, engaged in persecuting the Christians. How was he converted? Not by preaching, but by power – the power of the Holy Spirit, which threw him to the ground and blinded him. Through prayer and laying on of hands by Ananias, Paul's sight was restored. As we have seen, from that moment he served as a most faithful witness to Christ and performed many miracles.

Those who close their minds to the miracles performed by Jesus, will probably remain closed to those of Paul. We know that in every century there were saints and martyrs to whom the powers of discernment were given and through whom miracles were performed, right up to our own times. So, do miracles happen today? Time to move on to the next chapter.

Chapter 9

THE CHRISTIAN HEALING MINISTRY:
IN OUR TIMES

We have the teaching and example of Jesus and the successful ministry of Paul and the disciples to assist us in our ministry. All kinds of illness, deafness and blindness were healed, evil spirits were cast out and, occasionally, the dead were raised. We know how it was done – through prayer and laying on of hands, in the power of the Holy Spirit, and to the glory of God.

We have our Lord's command: 'Heal the sick.' How are we doing?

Although through the centuries many miracles of healing are recorded, particularly at holy shrines, it appears that until the early part of the twentieth century the Christian healing ministry was virtually unknown. It was assumed to have been just part of our Lord's ministry, powerfully continued by Paul and the disciples after Christ's ascension.

A large number of Christian churches throughout the land and in nearly all denominations all over the world now hold services of healing. Often these services take place in conjunction with the Eucharist, but they can be fitted in to any service and there are many appropriate hymns and readings available. Those officiating are usually the incumbent of the church and one or two trained lay people or other clergy. Towards the end of the service those in need of healing are invited to come forward and kneel at the sanctuary rail. They make known their problems to the person ministering and receive laying on of hands with prayer, which normally lasts not more than three minutes. Healing services can take place anywhere – cathedrals, churches, chapels, barns, halls and arenas. At Harnhill Christian Centre, near Cirencester, healing services take place weekly on Wednesday evenings in the barn and on Friday mornings with a Communion Service in the adjoining little church, attended by fifty to seventy people. Here there are eight to ten pairs of trained people ministering and each patient has the opportunity of explaining their personal problems and receiving advice as well as prayer. Burrswood Christian Centre, Groombridge, Kent, founded by Dorothy Kerin, also has weekly healing services in the lovely Church of Christ the Healer. The Old Rectory, Crowhurst, Battle, Sussex has weekly services of healing in their chapel, a modern hexagonal building with a deep sense of peace. Further details of the above Centres are in the Appendix.

In the time of our Lord's ministry, and that of Paul and the disciples, we are told again and again: 'They were all healed.' Those who come to healing services today – are they all healed? If not, why not? It is important to face up to this question and try to learn the lessons. Yes, there are several miraculous instant healings recorded at healing services and I have met some of those who have been healed. Although complete instant healings are not reported at every service, I believe that most of those coming forward do receive some blessing or benefit. It may be peace of mind, courage or a lessening of pain. If it were not so people would not continue to come to these services.

Nevertheless, we must not duck the question: 'Why are not all healed?' We are obeying our Lord's command to pray for the sick in His name and to glorify the Father. We work as channels for the power of the Holy Spirit. What is different from the disciples' ministry? Except for Paul, the disciples had been taught by Jesus and had witnessed His healings. We have absorbed the teaching on the subject, as recorded in the Gospels and in Acts, and it seems unlikely that there is some special ingredient that has been omitted. Faith is essential, both on the part of the person ministering and the patient. The following examples emphasise this. The father of a boy possessed of an evil spirit asked Jesus to cure him: 'If it is at all possible for you . . .' Jesus replied: 'Everything is possible to one who believes.' 'I believe; help my unbelief,' the father cried and the boy was healed (Mark 9:17–27). It was faith that led the woman with the issue of blood to touch the hem of Jesus' garment in order to receive healing (Mark 5:25–34). No words were spoken before the healing took place, but the woman knew at once that she had received healing and Jesus became aware that power had gone out of Him. He said to the woman: 'Your faith has healed you.'

Jesus knew the importance of faith on the part of the patient seeking healing. Even our Lord was unable to heal many people at Nazareth because of their lack of faith. 'Is he not the carpenter's son?' they said with scorn. Jesus responded: 'A prophet never lacks honour, except in his home town and in his own family' (Matthew 13:57).

Let us consider the circumstances in the Holy Land some two thousand years ago. There were no healing services, no sophisticated medicines, no clinics, hospitals, hospices or health service. If you were ill, lame, blind, deaf, in intolerable pain, possessed of evil spirits or had failing eyesight . . . just your bad luck! No hope. You were one of many. Then Jesus or a disciple appears and asks if you want to be made whole – and you are completely healed. Just like that! No wonder the people flocked to Him. Other sick people saw or heard of these miracles and went to Jesus expecting to be healed. They were desperate because there was no other way and this further sharpened their faith and expectancy. It is a fact that neither our Lord nor the disciples appear to have arranged healing services. They healed individually. It is interesting to note that some people were actually healed without personal ministry, through scarves and other items that had been blessed by Paul and taken to them.

I believe that individual ministry is important and some healing services give the opportunity for the patient, after the service, to inform the minister of any special problems or worries. It may well be that there is some emotional problem that needs to be attended to by inner healing and counselling before physical healing can take place. This is almost a 'mechanical' thing – blockages to healing are caused by such things as sin, guilt, fear, worry and resentment. Love and healing cannot flow when the mind is full of such impeding emotions. These must and can be removed by prayer and ministry before prayer for physical healing can be effective.

There is not an opportunity at a normal healing service for discussion with a patient on such details as inner healing. This requires individual ministry, which should be available in parishes. Mentioned elsewhere in this book is the Godalming Guild of Health Healing Prayer Group at Normanhurst, of which I was a member and which gave a full hour to each patient, with very positive results. There is certainly scope for such a group in every parish but, unfortunately, many clergy are not prepared to allow such a group to operate in their parish. If a group does operate, most clergy are too busy to join as a member.

A few churches have the splendid practice of offering healing ministry to individuals at the end of every service. This is normally done in side aisles in relaxed fashion, not in the sanctuary. For many years the Church of Holy Trinity, Brompton, which has done so much pioneering work in healing and evangelism, has regarded every service as a healing service.

At healing services we do encourage people to come up

for laying on of hands as proxy for a suffering relative or friend. The Reverend Jocelyn Grundy, when vicar of Fleet, experienced a number of these proxy healings. The wife of an alcoholic went to a healing service and, without her husband's knowledge, prayed for her husband's addiction. When she returned home she was greeted with the remark: 'I have stopped drinking' and this time he had stopped for good. At the same church a man with leukaemia, pronounced by the doctors as dying, was prayed for at the service by his wife. When she returned home he was out of bed and made a complete recovery. As we have seen in other cases, not only can one be healed without being present but also without having been informed that one is being prayed for.

We have established that healing services today do not usually result in the dramatic healings reported in the Gospels and Acts. Lack of expectancy, less faith and the many benefits of modern health care are contributing causes. We also have to face the fact that we are in a very materialist age, a climate that does not encourage dependence on God or miracles.

Although we are instructed, rightly so, that we must minister in pairs, never in our own name or our own strength, it is a fact that some people are blessed with the gift of healing. St Paul tells us this in 1 Corinthians 12:9 – 'Another, by the same Spirit, is granted . . . gifts of healing'. This does not mean that prayers for healing by a faithful believer will not be effective, but some will tend to be more effective than others. There are some people who are effective channels for healing a particular ailment, for example rheumatism or headaches. Those who do not possess gifts of healing will almost certainly possess equally important gifts, such as the gift of discernment. All gifts must be used to the glory of God. There should be no suggestion that the vicar should be the only person to lay on hands, but in many churches this is still the case.

Healing services have an important function in making Christian healing ministry available to all and many people are too shy to come for individual personal ministry. I may be in trouble for saying this, but although I am completely in favour of formal healing services, and have been involved in many, this is not always the most effective way to minister. I have attended really moving and meaningful healing services in cathedrals, churches and chapels and I would certainly never wish to deter anyone from holding or attending a healing service. However, healing services do not always provide the deep sense of peace and love which is conducive to healing.

The point is that healing ministry in the parishes should consist of much more than holding healing services and more attention needs to be given to Healing Prayer Groups and individual ministry. I have mentioned our Lord's love and compassion and it is our love and compassion that we have to minister in His name to the sick and troubled in the parish. It is important to have a list, regularly updated, of all those in the parish who are unwell. They will be prayed for regularly at the Eucharist and those who are in hospital should normally be offered a visit by a lay pastoral assistant or other member of the church. This does involve administration also.

It should be emphasised that all lay people serving in the healing ministry must receive training. This can be in the parish or diocese and there are excellent one-week courses, including those at Crowhurst, where long ago I did the introductory and advanced courses. These were most helpful and sensitively run.

I have heard it said, by a member of our congregation: 'If someone is healed, what does it matter whether the healer is Christian or not.' The answer is: 'You can only be made whole in body, mind and spirit through Jesus Christ.' The fact is that there are reported to be, at the start of the new millennium, some twenty thousand people in the UK who have set themselves up as 'healers'. Some are spiritualists, acknowledging a 'spirit guide' as the source of healing. They are potentially dangerous and definitely to be avoided. Some of them have Middle East royalty and show business personalities among their generous clients. There are others who say that their power is 'God-given' but who practise healing under their own name and build up a personal reputation. They are acting in disobedience of our Lord's rules for they do not give glory to God and most of them accept payment or gifts for their services. There is no linking of their ministry to a church, no back-up or support beyond themselves.

Sue and I have had personal experience of a 'healer'. We had a wonderful Christian friend, who was very ill with muscular dystrophy. She had great faith in a well-known faith healer, David, and she urged us to come to one of David's surgeries, which took place at her lovely house in Sussex.

There were about eight people sitting in the kitchen, which acted as a waiting room. Every ten minutes or so David would return to the kitchen with a patient, wash his hands at the sink, with his sleeves rolled up – I was forcibly reminded of a vet washing his hands and arms after an internal examination of a cow! David then returned to his allotted room with the next patient and so it went on. Sue and I made it clear that we had come to support our friend. When my turn came I was quite open with him and said that I was a member of the Christian healing ministry and was interested to learn more of his work. I was interested to learn how his ministry differed from ours. David did not pray aloud or refer to God but concentrated on making the patient feel at peace. He relied mainly on touch, touching with his hands over a wide area of the person and for a longer period than is normal in the church's ministry. David assured me that he does not find his work of healing tiring, partly because he does not pray aloud. This I can understand. Reverend Dr Martin Israel also lays on hands silently but the difference is that at the end he prays: 'In the name of the Father, the Son and the Holy Spirit, Amen,' making clear the source of the healing. David makes no mention of God and all the patients we spoke to had praise only for David. None mentioned God; 'Isn't David a wonderful healer . . .' Some months later I came across a book about David written by one of his patients. David contributes the final paragraph: 'At the end of it all, I found myself being certain only of God's love and wonder at the work that He requires of me – work that I, of myself, do not do but in which I am a channel for His loving kindness to all.' What a pity that David could not openly give the glory to God, rather than accept it for himself. Like many healers, he is a professional, relying solely on healing for his income.

No healer or non-Christian organisation can give the depth and breadth of quality service that Christian ministry provides. Healing encompasses wholeness of body, mind and spirit. It is not unusual for a physical illness, sometimes cancer, to follow some deep emotional experience such as divorce or bereavement – and inner healing through listening and prayer is needed before physical healing can take place.

I was given the autobiography of one of the best known occult healers. He called up the spirits of famous surgeons, long-since dead, and asked them to diagnose medical problems and suggest treatments for his patients. At one stage he spoke of his dead mother flying around his bedroom ceiling. The whole book was so creepy and horrible that I actually felt threatened and I put it on the fire. Unlike members of the Christian healing ministry, 'healers' are not renowned for humility and this one boasted of receiving from grateful, wealthy clients a portrait, a statue and a bust of himself, which are displayed in his clinic.

One can usually sense if someone is in contact with a healer. Sally was a lovely young mother, not a church member, who had contacted me. She had drastic surgery for her cancer and the surgeon told me afterwards that he had not expected her to survive more than forty-eight hours. I visited Sally regularly and prayed with her and she was in remission for several months. She was very brave and had a number of spells in hospital. One day I had the feeling that she was in touch with another healing source and Sally admitted to me that she was on the books of the Harry Edwards Healing Centre. I told her that I would withdraw, because it was not right to pray to the Lord for her healing if she was also under a 'healer'. This was my instinctive reaction and I still believe that it was the right one. Sally cried and implored me not to leave. She said she would ask to be taken off the other list. A short time later she remarked: 'The Lord's healing is so much purer.' And that was from someone who was not a church member. During one of Sally's spells in a nursing home I was due to go abroad for a three-day business visit. I was very reluctant to leave Sally and had considered putting off the business but she encouraged me to go. I phoned the visiting chaplain of the nursing home as I felt that as I should not be there it would be good if he could give Sally a little more time. I said I would be away for three days to which he responded: 'So what!' He was a first-rate and revered professional; it is understandable that he should have considered me as an intruding amateur and it was good for my humility. On my return from Europe I immediately telephoned Sally's husband to ask how she was and was shattered when he told me she had died. Recalling this has made me realise that many of our Lord's healings were performed through compassion and not only to give glory to God. Certainly in these early cases compassion was my main motive.

Looking back, I suppose it was somewhat incongruous that a sixty-year-old company chairman and past High Sheriff should regularly be visiting and praying with a young mother whom he had not previously met. I felt led to do so and I did go in the power of the Lord; it did not seem at all strange to me and I was welcomed by the husband and supported by Sue, although often she was not with me on these occasions. There is a spiritual dimension to life, which can override all things, but deep humility is essential.

Many parishes, including ours, also have a Healing Prayer Group which usually meets fortnightly, prays together for all the known sick people in the parish and arranges visiting for those in hospital.

I was also a founder member of the Godalming Guild of Health Prayer Group led by Mrs Peggy de Pemberton in her home. There were about eight of us of which at least six, including our splendid Christian doctor, Chris Jagger, and we met from 8.30 p.m. until about 10 p.m. Most of the patients were referred by Dr Chris and the first half-hour was taken up with briefing about the patient and prayer and meditation. There was only one patient each evening, sometimes a married couple. On arrival, at 9 p.m., the patient was welcomed and the programme explained. First, we asked the patient to tell us their problems or symptoms of illness, emphasising our confidentiality. We would then advise and ask questions after which prayer would follow and the patient would be offered the laying on of hands – always accepted. Apart from illness, including cancer, we had a wide range of problems brought to us including stress, marital, emotional, mental, occult, financial. The occult problem required special prayers for protection and we had an extra prayer team protecting us from another room. Bishop Morris Maddocks and his wife Anne happened to be with us that evening and they were very aware of the occult presence and the heat generated by it. God is not dead, but neither is the Evil One. I made notes on the sixty patients we saw and I only felt that three had not benefited, one was a giggling schoolgirl who did not know why she had come, and another assured us that all was well with her marriage, which sadly we knew to be untrue. It needs to be emphasised that in prayer and spiritual matters we must be completely open and truthful. There is no point in trying to hide anything from God.

We do need to be expectant and I was concerned at the attitude of an Anglican bishop who stated that: 'God will give some blessing and He knows best. We must not try to manipulate or impose our will on Him.' This does not, in my view, tie in with our Lord's: 'Ask and you will receive.' If we do not expect miracles, we shall not receive them. Our Lord does encourage us to expect miracles. If we do not believe that God has the power to work miracles we denigrate Him. Many of us have ample proof of miracles, which are seen daily all over the world. The more we expect and the more we honour Him, the more we are likely to receive, especially if we ask in humility and openness and with persistence. Through miracles God is glorified.

Pentecostal Christians claim many miracles. They expect miracles. They are positive, perhaps appearing to lack sensitivity but, in the power of the Holy Spirit, they expect God to heal. We can learn from them and apply their faith and expectancy with our brand of love and reverence.

Paul himself, that most dedicated servant of the Lord, did not receive the healing that he prayed for of the ailment described as 'a thorn in my flesh' (2 Corinthians 12:7–10). Three times he begged the Lord to rid him of it, but the answer came: 'My grace is all you need; power is most fully seen in weakness.' Paul was then happy to boast of his weakness because then the power of Christ would rest on him. It would be good if the Lord told us the reason when we do not receive healing. Have you thought of asking Him? Thinking about this, I am aware of being very fortunate in having excellent health. I have had two ailments for which I did not have ministry and I always assumed that God had granted me healing but I now realise that Sue and our chaplain knew of my problems and clearly had been praying, and I do give thanks. If we serve the Lord as wholeheartedly, night and day, as Paul did, or if we pray as fervently and listen as openly as he did, no doubt, like Paul, we would be given the answers. By the same token, if we reached the standards of dedication to God's will that permeated Paul and the other apostles, undoubtedly our healing ministry would be far more effective.

Refusal to forgive appears to be a complete barrier to healing. We had a testimony from a lady whose daughter suffered from anorexia and was then raped by her driving instructor and completely went to pieces. You can imagine the mother's feelings towards the rapist. God told her she must forgive him. 'I can't' she wailed. God responded: 'But you can if you really want to.' She did want to. Eventually she was given the power to meet the man, to completely forgive and embrace him and then the daughter was completely healed.

An unusual recent case is that of the well-known dedicated Christian and author Jennifer Rees-Larcombe. Jennifer and her husband had five children, she took on endless church work and she was one of those people who would never say 'No' to anyone needing help. The result was that she became very ill with a nervous complaint and spent some years in a wheelchair, often in great pain. Being an active Christian many of her friends were praying for her healing but there was no improvement. Some of these friends told Jennifer that she must be doing something to displease the Lord or He would heal her. One can imagine Jennifer's sense of frustration, but she was not resentful and accepted that it was evidently God's will that she should not be healed. Then she attended a healing service at Haslemere in Surrey, where she was to give the address. A newly converted Christian girl in her late teens told Jennifer that she believed that she would be healed. Jennifer then said that obviously she was the person who should pray for her healing. She had never done this before but, with Jennifer's encouragement, she did say a simple prayer for healing and Jennifer was able to get up out of her wheelchair and walk. She had been completely and permanently healed.

Obviously, it would be as wrong to suggest that prayers are never answered as that they are always answered in the way we hope. There are all sorts of reasons why prayers do not appear to be answered. It happens quite frequently that a prayer is answered in quite a different way to what was requested, but in fact, what is granted turns out to be better than what was requested. An obvious example is praying for someone to recover from a very serious illness in circumstances where a peaceful passing away would be better for the sick person and all concerned.

I am aware of one occasion when I had a strong conviction that my prayer for healing was being answered. It was many years ago and P. was desperately ill and near to death in hospital in the north. Of course, many others were also praying for her. At the end of my prayer, I was given the sudden definite awareness that she was going to recover. More than thirty years later P. came to lunch with us, when her husband was in hospital. Sue was in the kitchen and P. and I were talking by the fire in the dining room. We had met frequently in the intervening years but I had never mentioned to her the incident when she was so ill and I felt that prayers were being answered. This seemed the moment to mention it. 'Oh, but it was answered!' exclaimed P. with animation. 'The Lord took me by the hand and said: "You are going to get better" and, as you know, I did.'

There is another case where somebody for whom I prayed was healed although I had not told her that I was praying and she had not asked for prayer. Molly, who had been staying with us, had a particularly nasty cough and after she left I prayed for her healing. She lived near Coventry and it was some time before we met again and then she asked me if I had prayed for the healing of that cough. I said that I had and Molly then told me that it had suddenly been healed and she felt that somebody must have been praying and thought it was probably me. Believers will believe and cynics may doubt.

At a Guildford Cathedral Healing Service, a man prayed for his mother-in-law who was in considerable pain and lying in the Surrey County Hospital. When he visited her the next day in hospital she, knowing nothing about the healing service, said: 'At about 8.30 last night the pain suddenly went and has not returned.'

When, in spite of our prayers, healing does not take place, the fault may well be ours if we are not sufficiently in tune with our Lord and His Holy Spirit. As the Reverend Dennis Duncan reminds us, we need 'A closer walk with God.' Through contact with Christ, spiritual power increases, then: 'Nothing will be impossible for you.' Lack of full healing is not God's fault but ours, in not being sufficiently Christ-like and not being 'in Him'. It is right to be authoritative but equally right to be humble. One thing emphasised in the Church's ministry of healing is that we are merely channels of God's healing. We can do nothing of ourselves and, like the disciples, we operate only in His name and in the power of the Holy Spirit.

Although not a Roman Catholic, I do revere the Blessed Virgin Mary. Sue and I have visited two of the sites at which she has appeared, Fatima in Portugal and Knock in Ireland. We have not yet managed a visit to Lourdes but hope to do so. This is the place where St Bernadette had her vision of the Blessed Virgin Mary and where many miracles of healing have been granted. Even those not healed apparently do feel the great depth of spirituality and human caring. Mary Tanner told us of a visit to Lourdes with a friend who was very ill and for whom the medical profession had failed to find the cause. She was reluctant to go to Lourdes and, on the way home, there was still no improvement. 'I told you so,' she said triumphantly to Mary. 'Wait' was Mary's response. A few weeks later this lady collapsed when out walking near a London hospital. A passing pedestrian attended to her and eventually said that he knew what her problem was. He happened to be one of, I think, only three specialists in England who were expert in this particular medical problem and she was completely cured. Again, it is difficult to believe that this was mere coincidence.

Many people, like myself, have witnessed the 'power healing' ministry of the late John Wimber from the USA. He made a number of visits to the UK with his team and held healing sessions in large venues, such as Wembley, with thousands of people present. The day commenced with a number of repetitive hymns sung several times. There was then a talk, nearly always Bible-based. John was a very sound Christian minister, a close friend of the late Reverend David Watson and the London days were organised by the church of Holy Trinity, Brompton. John Wimber and his team had what is known as 'the gift of knowledge' to an impressive degree. He would say, for instance, 'There is someone sitting in the back row in that corner [pointing] who recently had a car accident and still has trouble with his right leg.' 'There is someone at the end of that middle row who is having great pain in her eyes and fears blindness . . .' They did not all respond immediately, but I think eventually they all did come forward. It was impressive. The people came up and received prayer and laying on of hands publicly in the arena. Many appeared to receive healing. I am certain that this was all genuine. John Wimber went on picking people out, listing, it seemed, all possible maladies and I was thankful not to be called. Then he said: 'Anyone with a stiff neck . . .' I really did have a stiff neck that day, so I went up. I did not have John Wimber ministering but two members of the church, a lady and a young man of about seventeen. The first thing he asked me was: 'Have you any connection with the occult?' which did not go down too well! He ended up by telling me that my nerves were in a pretty bad way and I had better have ministry from my own church when I got home. John Wimber had a splendid worldwide ministry and made many people aware of the reality of the power of God. He, and, in a rather different style, Francis MacNutt, have had a considerable influence worldwide, bringing awareness of God's healing in our times through their international ministries and the many books that they have written. Personally I tend to find these large and noisy gatherings stressful rather than peaceful, no doubt the cause of my stiff neck!

It is not generally known that animals as well as human beings are also healed through prayer. I have heard of dogs that were very ill being healed through prayer. I have also met, on a Christian healing course, an Irish lady who, with her husband, bred thoroughbred horses. She told us that she had often healed horses by prayer, sometimes when the vet was unable to help. On one occasion she and her husband were away when a valuable stallion suffered a very serious condition which the vet was unable to remedy. The animal was believed to be dying. The Irish grooms were very concerned and one of them said: 'If Missus were here she would pray, so we'd better do that.' They did and the horse immediately recovered. This may sound strange, but I regard the lady who told me as entirely dependable. Animals are part of God's creation and I see no reason why He should not be prepared to heal them if we have the faith to ask.

Animals, in fact, are much less likely to have psychological barriers to healing than human beings. I am sure that we are not alone in having known dogs, especially labradors, whose patient devotion to master or mistress is more than a match for the dedication shown by many of us humans to our Master. To which must be added at least one horse, Duncan.

There are a number of specialised areas in the Christian healing ministry. Although ministering and praying for any people in need of God's strength, guidance or healing, many of us feel guided to some particular sphere of the ministry, which in my case, with my wife Sue, is cancer.

Chapter 10

LOSELEY CHRISTIAN CANCER HELP CENTRE

I described in my book *The Loseley Challenge* how Dr Chris Jagger and I felt led to form this group at Loseley, in obedience to Bishop Morris Maddocks' instruction at the 1986 Acorn Christian Healing Conference that members should start up their own Christian healing initiatives in their own dioceses. Together with Chris Jagger, senior partner in a local medical practice and revered Christian, and myself, the other founder members were my wife Sue and Reverend Pat Ashe, our chaplain. We were privileged to have the support and encouragement of Bishop Morris and Anne Maddocks. With only minor alterations, the Loseley Christian Cancer Help Centre has continued for over fourteen years, without missing a single first or third Tuesday in any month. Only once, on a horrible day of freezing fog in the first year, have we not had at least one cancer patient for ministry. We have been richly blessed.

The current leaflet giving the programme and brief details is on the opposite page. It may be helpful to give some further details on the 2 p.m. session. I normally welcome everyone, especially newcomers, and give any information that may be appropriate, including announcing the leader of the afternoon session. This may be one of the Support Group or an invited speaker. As leaders we have been honoured to include three bishops, one on three occasions, Jennifer Rees-Larcombe the well-known

Above: The Sanctuary, St Nicholas Church, Compton.
Below: James and Sue More-Molyneux flanked by Dr. Chris Jagger (left) and the Rev. Pat Ashe, founder members of the Christian cancer group.

Opposite Page:
Top Left: The upper landing Cross and 1986 chapel, Loseley House.
Top Right: The east window of the chapel.
Below: The 1997 chapel, interior view.

Above: The chapel and Thomas More Room.
Right: 'The Living Christ' by Berthe Hess.

Jesus Christ by M. Brookfield King, 1928.

LOSELEY CHRISTIAN CANCER HELP CENTRE
in association with the
Acorn Christian Healing Trust

Any cancer patients and their carers are very welcome – of any denomination or none. The ministry they will receive is Christian – God's love and our love as his channels. The atmosphere is informal, warm and caring.

We meet in the Chapel and Tithe Barn on the Loseley House lawns on the first and third Tuesdays of each month.

Church ministers, of any denomination, and medics are welcome. Please telephone in advance.

An 18-minute video is available.

A Day for patients with Parkinson's disease is held, with the same programme, normally on the second Tuesday in February, May, August and November – please telephone beforehand to confirm.

For further information, please telephone James or Sue on 01483 566090. Also anyone ill at home or in hospital wishing to be visited or prayed for, please telephone Melody on 01483 835207.

No charges are made

Programme
Music in the Chapel from 12 noon

12.30 pm **Optional Eucharist** including laying on of hands for any desiring it. Please arrive by 12.20 pm if attending the Eurcharist

1.15 pm **Lunch.** Please bring sandwiches and we will provide tea and coffee.

2.00 pm **Welcome, relaxation, hymns, prayer, reading, sharing.** Prayer and laying on of hands for those who were unable to be present earlier.

3.45 pm **Depart.** Some patients tire quickly: anyone may leave at any time.

On the third Tuesday in January, April, July and October, the sacrament of Anointing is offered at the Eucharist.

Loseley Christian Trust
Loseley Park
Guildford
Surrey GU3 1HS
Telephone: 01483 566090

Christian author and Elizabeth Austin, gifted American evangelist. We are frequently led by one of our patients, the Reverend Michael Baggott, an Anglican priest seriously ill with cancer, who is a great inspiration to us, also bereaved member Dawn Inwood and other members of the Support Group. Following the introductions I hand over to Dr Chris Jagger who gets us started singing hymns accompanied by his guitar and some relaxation exercises, as he feels appropriate. Chris is very gifted, not only medically and musically, but also in extempore prayer and he is a great support for whoever leads. We then have a short talk by the leader, followed by more songs, then perhaps prayer or a short Bible reading or meditation as the leader may decide. Sharing follows, started by Melody, our staff member, giving news of patients unable to be with us, then the patients tell us the good news and the bad about their progress and treatments. Then perhaps another song and we end by holding hands in a circle and saying the Grace together.

I have often remarked that it is the patients themselves, with their cheerfulness and serenity, who do most to impress and encourage newcomers. They certainly impress us in the Support Group. In addition to the founders, the Support Group consists of our current chaplain, Canon Dr Peter Thompson, the Reverend Professor Edward Williams and a dozen others including our only staff member, Mrs Melody Crawt.

Melody, a dedicated Christian filled with compassion, came to us after sixteen years' nursing experience. She is the ideal person to keep in touch with patients, ensuring that those requiring visits are visited, sending cards as appropriate, remembering anniversaries and keeping Sue and I informed about those who are going through a bad time or about to have an operation. These are Melody's priorities and she also looks after such details as preparing the chapel for services and helping with administration. In the summer season, when Loseley is open to the public, Melody does splendid work helping with showing videos and talking to visitors about our Christian ministry, making available books and cards and organising volunteers to help. It would fill several chapters to attempt to list the attributes of all the Support Group members. They are a splendid bunch of dedicated, compassionate Christians – Catholics, Baptists, evangelicals and Anglicans – all united in compassion and in the cause of Christ. In the background, unseen by members, is the Loseley secretary, Nicola, the paragon who deals with all correspondence, records and accounts.

It is not possible to convey the very special atmosphere at our meetings to anyone who has not actually attended, but the following comments made by members may help. After the death of one much-loved member, her daughter wrote. 'Mum loved going to Loseley. She said she didn't know what she'd do without it . . . The moment she entered your gates something special happened and whatever you talked about in your discussions was exactly pertinent to her. She so appreciated the kindness, generosity, support . . . Please keep her in your prayers.' We do keep her in our prayers and all our members who have passed on are individually remembered in the Chapel every Sunday as well as at Thanksgiving and Remembrance Day held for bereaved members every April.

The following testimonies are drawn from earlier years, some from my book *The Loseley Challenge*. They are representative of many more people, equally courageous and dependent on God. Annette, Keith's wife from Hayling Island, had been pronounced as terminally ill when she first came to us, with breast cancer having spread to her duodenum and liver. A few years later Annette gave her testimony on our original video. She told how she had received the Holy Spirit when hands were laid on her at

Loseley. Soon afterwards she was found to be clear of cancer. The specialist said: 'You're fine – what's your secret?' Shy as she was, that was one secret that Annette would always be happy to divulge. Very sadly, two years later she had a fatal relapse and is deeply mourned.

Andrew was a churchwarden in his seventies, retired, recently widowed and seriously ill with lung cancer. The first time that he came to Loseley was 9th October 1987, a few days after the hurricane, and he was one of the most dejected human beings we had ever encountered. Because of the storm, our numbers were down and Andrew cast a deep spell of gloom on us all. At the next meeting he was a little brighter and, after that, he was a new person. From then on Andrew was always cheerful and uncomplaining, and a wonderful example to us all, despite horrendous bouts of coughing. He had more than a year in remission, then one day he turned to me and said, quite casually: 'I'd be awfully grateful if you would read the lesson at my funeral.' He died the following week and I was happy to fulfil his request. When he had joined us Andrew was, understandably, immersed in his own woes of lung cancer and the loss of his wife after a long and happy marriage. He was a dutiful Christian and churchwarden, yet he had not yet discovered God at a deeper personal level. It was in meeting patients at Loseley, who were also suffering but who had found peace and strength through the power and love of God, that Andrew was led to discover their secret. God is so much more than the Church. That is one of my main themes, but it must always be emphasised that the Church is not redundant and that it is essential that Christians join together to worship and glorify God.

Among our early members were a lovely couple, Tony and Anne. After joining the group, Tony was healed of two cancers and seemed to be cured. He also received an 'inner healing' of emotional problems at Loseley. Very sadly, Tony then died from an inoperable brain tumour. Years later his widow Anne remarried; the new husband was the widower of Maureen, another of our lovely patients. We have all been inspired and uplifted by the wonderful courage and faith of so many patients. Others include Vera, who, a week before she died, testified on video to the great peace that she had received: 'I can relax now, I couldn't before.' And Mildred: 'Nothing with the Lord is terminal. His love is eternal . . . We know that He is in tomorrow. There is nothing to fear.'

Kit, an indomitable Irish lady, lived alone with her ancient labrador, Ben. She was riddled with pain, rheumatism, cancer and diabetes, yet always cheerful. A devout Catholic, she was always giving thanks to God and giving gifts to all who visited. Laurie, another patient, shared with his wife Dawn a deep faith and dependence on God. He issued a periodical newsletter, short extracts of which are given below:

> Ever since my illness began I have felt the close presence of the Lord. From the start I had this wonderful feeling that all my sins are forgiven. Joy filled my whole body and the wonderful peace is still with me every day. I have come closer to the Lord . . . Also, a deep desire to praise Him for all He does for me. When I walk in the village, many friends come up to me for a chat. We always talk about prayer in the High Street, both with churchgoers and non-churchgoers.

Lawrie and Dawn were a wonderful encouragement to us all and when, very sadly, the cancer finally took Lawrie in 1993, Dawn came to the very next meeting as a member of the Support Group and has been coming ever since and often leads us.

In all these years, we have never heard any patient complain: 'Why does it have to happen to me?' but 'Praise the Lord' is frequently heard. We remember eleven-year-old Sarah, determined to come again, even though too weak to walk from room to room, and Christine who arrived on her last visit to Loseley by ambulance on a stretcher. Knowing that she had not long to live, she insisted on taking the family to Disneyland, Florida, and died at peace soon afterwards. Father Peter OFM, from Chilworth Franciscan Friary never complained although suffering long and painfully.

I have nothing but admiration for over one hundred and twenty patients who have passed on and those who are included in these pages represent them all. The following are some quotations from recent members who feature on our latest video.

Noel: When the diagnosis came, not only had I got prostate cancer but I had also got bone hot spots which meant that I wasn't able to have the operation which could have put a stop to it – it was too late. So we went to Loseley without really knowing much about it. We hadn't even been to the House. At Loseley we find what we find nowhere else, we find the real support and the long-term answers and real comfort and joy and if I go feeling really low and depressed, I come away feeling tremendously cheered. Really very greatly helped. There seems to be a wonderful atmosphere of love at Loseley, you can almost touch it. I was absolutely amazed because we are asked to share and the microphone is passed around from one to another and you would have thought that with fifty people there would be a good deal of nervousness and people wouldn't really feel free to tell what they were really feeling, but there is such an enfolding of support and fellowship that it is the opposite. People probably say more in those sharing sessions than they would say to friends or even possibly their spouses.

Nell: Yes, as a carer one does feel very emotional about your partner. We've been together a long time.

Pam: I have been totally healed by the word of Jesus and by the prayer and by the support of everybody. I thank Jesus, thank God, thank everybody because never once, after I'd got over my initial shock, have I ever felt alone, even at night when I woke up slightly anxious I would say: 'I'm in your arms Lord, care for me.' And I just never felt alone.

Judy, carer: Loseley has helped us enormously. I can remember when we first came saying we were meant to come here because the love and the care that we have both received here has been like nothing we've found anywhere else, and the wonderful people we've met here have just become our family and the support and the strength that we get from this is just terrific. One of the hardest parts of being the carer for a cancer patient was in the beginning, when he was first diagnosed with cancer. I wasn't expecting that and it really hit both of us between the eyes. And then, as time went on, you became able to deal with it a bit more easily. And then, when he went secondary, I found that was just as bad. It was the same problem to deal with again. Since the diagnosis, I think it's drawn us closer together and it's made us even closer to our family than we were before.

Bill: I've been a prostate cancer man for ten years now and I've been coming to Loseley for six years. One comes not just to receive but also to give and I think, having had quite a lot of experience of prostate cancer and the treatments for it, I can help other people with the same sort of problem and tell them of my experiences.

No one on the Support Group, except our caring professional visitor and helper, receives any remuneration. It is a matter for thanksgiving that we have such a close relationship with one another, united in our work for the Lord and the patients.

It should be emphasised that we are open to anyone with cancer. Sally had not been to church for years and it was a joy to have a telephone call from her when she got home from her first visit to us: 'I felt a great wall of love,' she said.

One day I remarked that I could not understand why God granted remissions, but allowed the patient eventually to die of cancer. This happened so often and I referred to the case of Jenny. Lovely Jenny had come to us two years before, very ill and with failing sight. The first Christmas she was not able to see our Christmas tree but the next year she could and was so thrilled that her vision was restored. Jenny received healing of further secondaries but not long afterwards became very ill again and died. Why did God heal twice and then allow her to die of cancer? Bill, a retired RN Commander and his wife Judy are wonderful Christians and Bill is so positive and cheerful that it is difficult to remember that he is a patient. It was he who answered the question: 'James, nothing is wasted. When she first came, Jenny, a Christian, feared death. She was not ready to die but she grew in faith, love and awareness of God and when the time came she was ready to say: "Thy will be done."' Jenny was very special and loved by all. After a difficult childhood she overcame many problems and had a wonderful and supportive husband, Roy. Roy, as a number of bereaved spouses, still sometimes joins us at our meetings and brings other members from the Redhill area.

Once a year, we have a Thanksgiving and Remembrance

Day, commencing with the Eucharist in chapel, at which the names of all those who have passed on are remembered. As with the normal cancer group Tuesdays, lunch in the barn follows and then we have about four quite short talks, the first by an outside speaker. These have included two bishops, one of whom was recently bereaved, Jennifer Rees-Larcombe and Dr Gareth Tuckwell, former director of Burrswood. The other speakers are drawn from our own bereaved members. Of course, there is an underlying sadness and a few tears, but the overall atmosphere is uplifting and of thankfulness to God. One letter mentioned: 'I have never felt such nearness.' Naturally, nearly all those present have been to the cancer Tuesdays in earlier days with their spouses and know the Support Group members as well as many of the other bereaved members present. The chapel and barn are familiar to them and they receive here what they always received, love and compassion and awareness of God.

It cannot be emphasised too strongly that our Christian ministry is not an alternative to medical treatment, but supplementary to it. Benefits of Christian ministry include a real sense of peace, which greatly improves the quality of life for both the patient and family. Sometimes there is pain relief and freedom from the side-effects of chemotherapy. Many long remissions have been granted – some patients coming with a life expectancy of just a few weeks have been given years.

Christian ministry is not primarily about instant physical healings but these do occur. Two ladies who have received instant miraculous healings have visited Loseley and given their testimonies to the group. Sue Coles, at the age of twenty-nine, had a malignant tumour removed from her colon. She has written her testimony of healing:

Four years later I gave birth to a third daughter and very soon afterwards I was found to have another growth and following major surgery underwent months of radiotherapy and chemotherapy. Then my life was shattered: another growth had shown up on an x-ray. I had faith in God and I prayed and my church prayed too. My dearest friend Krystyna, an unbeliever, watched, comforted and helped but what could she do to heal me? She had to turn to the Lord and pray. I was taken to an Anglican healing service in Hounslow. That evening I knew that I had been healed – I heard a heavenly choir singing and Jesus became very real. The day of the appointment with the consultant came – the lump had disappeared. Thank you Lord for healing me.

That was now over twenty years ago and there have been no further problems. Judith MacNutt visited us with her husband Francis, well-known internationally for his Christian healing ministry, his teaching and for his many authoritative books on the subject of Christian healing. It was a special day on which we also had as our guests some members from a self-help Cancer Group. Judith gave her testimony. In her early twenties she had been diagnosed as suffering from cancer in her womb and she was informed that a hysterectomy was imperative. She declined; she wanted to have children and she believed that God would heal her. A short time afterwards Judith received the laying-on of hands from a monk, Father Francis MacNutt. She felt tremendous heat, a common phenomenon, and believed that she had been healed. The healing was confirmed by the specialist and there were no more problems. It would be more accurate to record that there were no more medical problems, because there was a very big problem: Judith and the monk, the channel for her divine healing, had fallen in love. Eventually, Father Francis MacNutt withdrew from his monastic Order, he and Judith married and here they were with their two fine children. Francis and Judith head a renowned worldwide Christian healing and teaching ministry and it was through more splendid 'coincidences' that we were given this opportunity of their visit and of hearing Judith's testimony first-hand.

I should emphasise that LCCHC is not just about first and third Tuesdays. That is when we meet, but members in hospital receive visits and cards as well as being prayed for. All the members are prayed for in chapel every Monday, with daily prayers for those very ill. Bob, one of our splendid Support Group members, is our unpaid technical director, and has organised a simple and effective sound system for our meetings in the barn. He produces sheets of photographs of all our patients which are issued to all patients and Support Group members so that we can remember the individuals as we pray for them. As well as our members, at the present time we also have over seventy associate members, as far away as Australia, Canada and the USA, Ireland and Scotland. We pray for them regularly.

For the first ten years the Christian Cancer Centre operated in Loseley House. This was a lovely setting, but the chapel was up two flights of stairs on the top floor, not ideal for people who were very ill. As a result we sometimes had to use the drawing room for the Eucharist instead of the chapel.

In 1995 our son Mike, with Sarah and their children, Alexander, Katrina, Christopher and Tristram, swapped accommodation with Sue and I and moved into the main house, and we took over the nursery wing. This presented a problem for the Cancer Group, particularly as Mike frequently needed to let out the main rooms for seminars, filming, banquets and, later, for civil weddings. It was Mike who suggested the tithe barn and kindly offered it for our Tuesdays. This was ideal. We now had car park, restaurant, toilets and meeting room all on one level; so much easier for the patients than the multi-level elegance of the Elizabethan house, with its one WC up a difficult flight of steps! We had our Eucharist at one end of the tithe barn and then moved to the other end for lunch, and back to where the Eucharist had been held for the afternoon session. The tithe barn is originally seventeenth century, and was taken down piece by piece from a farm half a mile away and re-erected on the initiative, direction and energy of Fred Gooch, my recent business partner and one-time Loseley maintenance foreman. The barn is lovely and well heated, but we did miss the glorious peace of the little chapel in the House. We therefore applied to build a new chapel adjoining the barn. The horrified lady planning officer asked: 'What do you want a chapel for? . . . The problem is that you are in the green belt.' Every possibility was explored but after several months and inviting members of the Planning Committee individually to come to Loseley and hear and see what we were doing and why the chapel was needed, we finally got consent.

The building of that chapel I regard as one of the most satisfying projects with which I have ever been involved. Our architect, John Bennett, and his wife are Christian Scientists and my firm Guildway had produced a number of chapels for John. We chose a small builder, who had previously done some excellent work for Loseley, Ivan King. I chaired the Building Committee composed of Ivan, our chaplain the Reverend Pat Ashe and Fred Gooch, with the architect and Sue, my wife attending when appropriate. In addition to the meetings there was much prayer and thought on all the details. Ivan King is a superb and knowledgeable craftsman of independent mind. At the first meeting of the Committee he and I had a serious confrontation but, after this, we respected and understood one another and things could not have run more smoothly.

Everyone was really keen and dedicated. Fred and I have many years experience together in the building industry – though I cannot match Fred's whole life experience – but we have never before experienced such harmony between client, architect and builder as was manifested throughout the building of the chapel. There was much prayer and thought going on in the background and Sue and I visited a number of churches and chapels, making special journeys as far afield as Exeter to look at details. Our architect was also brilliant and among many other suggestions proposed a stone-tiled floor, much more in keeping with the ancient churches and cathedrals than our proposed wood flooring. I had long held the idea for the East window of a realistic dove, with feathers, descending in a path of glory. The stained glass artist we had selected for the windows declined to paint a real dove as that was sentimental. Fortunately, John knew a bird artist in the Isles of Scilly. We arranged for her to come up for briefing and we are all delighted with the result from a design by Fenella Bennett, wife of the architect. Nearly all the oak in the building was from Loseley, with four stanchions purchased from Compton church. Our retired maintenance foreman Larry Sheppard made the large five-foot cross on the east wall and Guildway and Loseley craftsman Peter Bridger made the sanctuary rail, the lectern, the pew and the cupboards. The West window – 'My peace I leave with you' – is the work of Caroline Benyon of the Carl Edwards Studio, which also supplied the mouth-blown glass in the clear windows.

Everyone worked with enthusiasm, not least builder Ivan and his son Dave. Even the consultant on the sound system realised that the chapel was something special and went to endless pains to ensure that we had the quality of sound to match it. The sanctuary carpet, specially woven in Nepal, was donated by Adam Gilchrist. Several chairs have been donated by bereaved families in memoriam. We are most grateful to all who have been involved in building and furnishing the chapel.

'My peace I leave with you' seemed the most appropriate

message in the West window from the Lord for people leaving after receiving healing ministry. The North window, featuring the Lamb, is funded by friends in the Surrey Lieutenancy to mark my retirement as Vice Lord Lieutenant of Surrey in 1996. The lectern Bible was presented by Sue. It is the Revised English Bible and Archbishop Donald Coggan, the Chairman of the Joint Committee that produced this version, kindly signed it for us.

A number of people asked to whom the chapel would be dedicated, perhaps to St Thomas More or St Francis? I gave the answer that it would just be the Loseley Chapel. One day, when it was nearing completion, it came to me quite clearly that it was to be dedicated 'To The Glory Of God', and so it was, by the Bishop of Guildford at a Eucharist on 25th March 1997. Pat Ashe, our chaplain assisted at the Eucharist, which was attended by sixty invited guests including the architect, builders, main craftsmen and donors.

The first and third Tuesdays of each month are for cancer patients and their carers only. We also hold quarterly days for Parkinson's disease patients. These follow exactly the same format as the cancer days – Eucharist and ministry, lunch and afternoon session, which is usually led by Dr Jagger. We can also arrange ministry in the chapel for anyone requiring prayer for healing. On these occasions we have a rule that there will be a minimum of two people ministering, and where possible one will be an ordained minister.

I should not leave the subject of Christian ministry to cancer patients without making clear our position, first in relation to the medical profession and then to self-help groups, holistic groups and 'healers'. There is a great deal of misunderstanding and people are discouraged from seeking God's healing through misinformation.

The Christian healing ministry accepts, fully supports

and uses the medical profession. They are an absolute necessity and in tending the sick they are doing God's work. St Luke was known as 'the beloved physician'. The Loseley Christian Cancer Help Centre co-founder, Dr Chris Jagger, is senior partner in a local medical practice. Our current chaplain, Canon Dr Peter Thompson, is also a qualified doctor, as is the Reverend Professor Edward Williams, another member of our Support Group. There are denominations that do not avail themselves of the services of the medical profession, but nearly all do and we seek to work together in harmony with the profession.

Sadly, there are still many GPs who look upon Christian ministry as something to be avoided. It is a fact that there are not many Christian Cancer Help Centres and, of the five I have known, three have had to close because of lack of patients. It appears that local doctors tend to advise patients against going to a Christian centre: 'They'll tell you that God will heal you. He won't and they will say it's your fault for not having enough faith. Stay with us and we'll look after you . . .' We would never dream of saying such things to any patient, either questioning faith or making them feel guilty.

There are many cancer self-help groups, which do splendid work in counselling and advising patients, giving sympathy, support and understanding. Members of such groups sometimes come to our meetings and they are most welcome. Some of the people running self-help groups are Christians but do not themselves undertake Christian healing ministry.

In recent years several splendid help centres have been established, usually within a hospital curtilege, professionally staffed and well equipped. These are often under the auspices of Macmillan or a similar organisation and funded by local charities. Such centres exist to help, advise, comfort and support patients. The local centre is happy to stock our leaflets and is sympathetic to our ministry.

I personally am very concerned at certain aspects of the holistic movement. Sue and I have been keen for fifty years on organic growing and involved with natural additive-free products, so holistic cancer treatment sounded good. But we were in for a shock. A leaflet *New Approaches To Cancer* is issued by St Peter's Hospital, Chertsey, Surrey together with a video. This contains a great deal of helpful information and advice, but then the comment is made: 'We also recommend healing (sometimes called "the laying-on of hands" or "spiritual healing") as this has been found to be very beneficial by most patients.' Christians must be concerned, however, at these further statements: 'It is not necessarily related to any belief system, nor does it require the patient to believe in anything, only to be open-minded.' The video actually shows three open-minded women laying-on hands; two are chatting and one is laughing. The Christian healing ministry is most anxious not to decry the efforts of any organisation that is helping patients – and there are many. However, I personally believe that it is important that people should be aware of false doctrines that denigrate Almighty God.

The literature of another well-known organisation which helps cancer patients has in recent years notably avoided any mention of the Almighty. A long time ago we had a visit from the representative of this same Cancer Centre. I asked him what they did for people who are dying. His immediate response was a passionate: 'Oh we don't want them to die!' Many people are being helped at this centre, staffed by dedicated, caring people, who believe that they are doing their best for their patients. The fact is that without Almighty God they miss out on the vital dimension for complete healing. Our patients can testify to the reality of the depth of the peace and love of God and the difference this makes. To make Him better known and loved: that is the motivation behind this book. We must use our earthly gifts and facilities to help those who are sick, but through Almighty God we have recourse to a deeper dimension, containing riches beyond price, at no cost other than being open to God in Christ Jesus.

Hospices provide the ultimate care for the terminally ill and their work is beyond praise. I have been privileged to be associated with the Phyllis Tuckwell Hospice at Farnham from the beginning and have seen it improve, year by year, in standards of care and facilities. Like many hospices, it has a lovely little chapel and a visiting chaplain. More and more hospices are being set up through local initiatives, the dedicated work of individuals and generous giving by many local people.

Dean Bridges, at a Guildford Cathedral service I attended years ago, preached about 'The Good Shepherd', pictured with a dear little lamb on his shoulder. Typically, the dean added: 'Actually, Middle East lambs are rather smelly and dirty, but the Shepherd saved it. All a sheep can do, if it gets lost or in trouble, is to bleat, to say: "Baa". We must learn to have the humility to bleat and God will hear us. Even if your wife is dying of cancer, He will hear and give you peace.'

Whatever patients' expectations may be when they come to Loseley, they are in fact bringing themselves and their troubles to God. And He does hear them. He hears too the cries of the bereaved, as we shall see in the next chapter.

Chapter 11

BEREAVEMENT AND ETERNAL LIFE

'Dear Lord, support us all the day long of this troublous life, until the shades lengthen and the evening comes, the busy world is hushed, the fever of life is over and our work is done. Then, Lord, in thy mercy grant us safe lodging, a holy rest and peace at the last. Amen.'
(Cardinal Newman. From Sermon
'Wisdom and Innocence')

Understandably, people find it difficult to speak of eternal life, but we all hope and a Christian expects. If we do not believe in this great gift, then we do not believe Jesus Christ. St Peter writes: 'Praised be the God and Father of our Lord Jesus Christ! In his great mercy by the resurrection of Jesus Christ from the dead, he gave us new birth into a living hope, the hope of an inheritance, reserved in Heaven for you, which nothing can destroy or spoil or wither' (1 Peter 1:3–4).

We must face it; we cannot just say 'death is nothing at all'. For the family and all close to the one who is no longer with them, the loss is traumatic and devastating. Even Jesus wept at the death of Lazarus, although one senses that it was the distress of the sisters, Mary and Martha, that caused his tears and moved him to raise Lazarus from the dead. Jesus understands and has compassion for our sorrows and we can take our grief to him in prayer. There are many books on helping and counselling the bereaved.

The offer of eternal life is a gift so gloriously precious that it is strange and sad that many people appear disinterested. The Christian has the great advantage over the unbeliever in knowing that separation is only temporary. St Paul's words are worth repeating: 'The wages of sin is death but the gift of God is eternal life through Jesus Christ Our Lord.' This is our true hope and faith. Apart from acceptance of our Lord's assurance, which should suffice, there are many other reasons for believing in the reality of eternal life. I have earlier emphasised the important fact that we all are body, mind and spirit. It is, of course, the spirit that goes on into eternal life. There is a whole company of Heaven including angels and archangels. Angels have many times been seen at the moment of death. Down the centuries, countless Christians were content to be horrendously tortured and killed because they were aware that they were headed for eternal life. Many need only have denied Christ to be spared. Such faith and conviction must be an encouragement to all who seek eternal life. Anyone who watched the televised funeral of Cardinal Basil Hume can hardly have doubted but that this very holy man was headed for his 'Master's Kingdom'. We give thanks for his life, humility and example.

There are people who have had near-death experiences, and who are aware of the reality of Heaven. Larry, who made the crosses both on the house staircase and in the new chapel, is one who nearly died at the age of five. He recalls being at the edge of Heaven with a little girl. The girl went through the gates of Heaven calling him to follow, but Larry replied: 'No, I must go back' and he survived and was restored to full health. I had known Larry for a long time before he told me this story. He normally only mentions it to people who are bereaved in order to help them to a belief in life hereafter. Larry is a wonderful, kind and compassionate person who does not consider himself religious.

The Spark of God

Not a great number of people have heard of Larry, but this cannot be said of Dorothy Kerin about whom many books have been written. Dorothy Kerin has said: 'I dare to say to you in the presence of God and all the company of Heaven that I have seen Jesus. I have heard His voice, I have felt His touch and I know that Jesus Christ is the same yesterday and today and forever.' Dorothy had been seriously ill for some years and the final diagnosis was of tubercular meningitis. For the last two weeks all treatment had been stopped. Dorothy had become delirious, blind and deaf and on 17th February the doctor told her mother that if any relations wanted to see Dorothy alive, they must be sent for at once for she could not live through the next day. He also commented that Dorothy had suffered enough to kill half a dozen people. On the next day, 18th February, several relatives did come. The dying girl's face was radiant, reflecting the glory of God. She had passed into the courts of Heaven:

I seemed to drift into space. I was no longer conscious of my body, but my soul was overflowing with joy and love and a transcendent feeling of supreme happiness, impossible to describe. I passed on and on, and as I went the way grew brighter and brighter, until I saw in front of me a wonderful altar formed by angels. There were six at the back, and in front one more beautiful than the rest holding a chalice, which she brought to me, and from which she gave me to drink. Then they disappeared, and as they went they seemed to be chanting words which I could not understand. I passed on again, and soon I heard a great flocking sound, and saw coming from every direction white-robed figures, some of them carrying lilies, while some had halos. Their movements made lovely music and they all looked as though they were coming and going with some definite purpose. No words of mine can exaggerate the exquisite beauty of the scene. As I looked I saw one coming towards me; I thought He was coming for me, and held out my hand towards Him, but He smiled and said: 'No, Dorothy, you are not coming in'.

Again I passed on, and this time I seemed to go a much greater distance, until I could go no further, when I heard a voice saying: 'Dorothy' three times. I answered: 'Yes, I am listening. Who is it?' Then a great light came all around me, and an angel took my hands in his and said: 'Dorothy, your sufferings are over. Get up and walk.' He passed his hands over my eyes and touched my ears, and then I opened my eyes and found myself sitting up in bed. My mother and a number of friends were standing round the bed, looking very frightened, and some clutching at each other. It seemed so strange to me, and I could not understand why they were all there. I asked for my dressing gown, telling them that I was quite well, and that I must get up and walk; but they were all too astonished to answer me or to move.

The angel again said to me: 'Get up and walk.' Then they brought the dressing gown and when I put it on I got out of bed unassisted. Part of the light came to the right side of the bed, and I put my hand on it, and it led me out of the room and along a passage and then back into my room again. Though I had not walked for five years, I now walked quite steadily, and was not the least bit shaky; indeed I felt so well and strong that I might never have been ill at all. Very soon I realised that I was hungry, and asked for food. They brought me milk in a feeding-cup, but I refused it, and finally I went down myself the two flights of stairs to the larder and brought back the materials for a real meal of meat and pudding. How I enjoyed that meal! It was the first solid food I had been able to digest for years, and I had not the slightest pain or discomfort after it.

Sixteen people were in the room, and all were mystified and amazed at what they saw. I was perfectly well, all the pain had left me, my sight was restored, and I felt better and stronger than I can ever remember feeling before. It was half past nine in the evening when I got up, and at twelve o'clock midnight, I went back to bed and slept until eight o'clock the following morning.

When the doctor called, expecting to sign the death certificate, he was utterly amazed when the patient ran to greet him. He asked her if she had climbed the stairs and she ran up two flights. Bishop Maddocks, in his book *The Vision of Dorothy Kerin*, states that in all probability Dorothy went as far on this journey as any have gone who eventually returned. The experience she related seems to describe the courts of Heaven, which on this earth we can only faintly imagine. But she did experience them.

Certainly, Dorothy Kerin is one who was able to believe in eternal life and her experience must be an encouragement to us all. Understandably, the press soon got hold of this miraculous event and, even in 1912, the family was besieged by reporters and journalists, so much so that Dorothy had to be whisked away to a secret address. There are similarities here with our Lord's healing of Jairus' daughter. I am very struck by the fact that after he had raised Jairus' daughter from the dead, Jesus commanded two things, first that she should be brought something to eat. This was also Dorothy's first need and she herself stated that she went down and collected a good meal. In the case of Jairus' daughter, our Lord's second command was that no one should hear of it. I had thought that this was rather strange, for if one had raised someone from the dead it would be an opportunity to glorify God; however, Jesus knew that people would flock to see this girl and would make the family's life a misery. So, in fact, the two needful things for Dorothy Kerin's aftercare were exactly what our Lord had prescribed for Jairus' daughter nearly 2,000 years before. This merits pause for reflection.

After her healing, Dorothy Kerin obeyed her Lord and founded a Home for Christian Healing, which moved to Burrswood in East Sussex in 1948. Burrswood flourishes today, greatly expanded under its previous director Dr Gareth Tuckwell and now Dr Michael Harper, with a dedicated Christian staff and community. Dorothy was aware that she had been restored to life and health for a purpose – to help to rekindle our Lord's ministry of healing.

'God so loved the world, that he gave his only Son, that everyone who has faith in him may not perish but have eternal life' (John 3:16). These words were spoken by our Lord and here lies the foundation for our hope of eternal life. Those who truly believe in the Lord will love and obey him. No one is completely without sin but those who confess their sins and truly repent have the assurance of forgiveness.

Included in the 'Sermon on the Mount' our Lord gives this important teaching:

> Do not store up for yourselves treasure on earth, where moth and rust destroy, and thieves break in and steal; but store up treasure in Heaven, where neither moth nor rust will destroy, nor thieves break in and steal. For where your treasure is, there will your heart be also.
>
> (Matthew 6:19–21)

Many of us have friends who have died and who, sadly, did not appear to have been storing up treasure in Heaven. There was an occasion when I quoted to a bereaved wife: 'Death hides, it does not divide; thou art on Christ's other side.' She responded: 'But sadly he wasn't a believer.' In these cases it is not for us to judge, we can still pray for them and our God is merciful. We can all gain encouragement from our Lord's words to one of the criminals crucified with Him:

> One taunted: 'Are not you the Messiah? Save yourself, and us.' But the other rebuked him: 'Have you no fear of God? You are under the same sentence as he is. In our case it is plain justice; we are paying the price for our misdeeds. But this man has done nothing wrong.' And he said, 'Jesus, remember me when you come to your throne.' Jesus answered, 'Truly I tell you: today you will be with me in Paradise.'
>
> (Luke 23: 39–43)

I believe that we should regard eternal life as God's gift – which it certainly is – rather than as a right. We can never claim to have earned it.

Just after my experience of the Holy Spirit at Bronwen Astor's prayer group (Chapter 4) I had three vivid and significant dreams, on successive nights. In one dream I was praying and aware of a wonderful atmosphere of peace and love. In the next dream many people were arriving at home for some form of Christian ministry in which I was involved. In the third and much the most powerful dream, I was dying. This was the best dream that I have ever experienced, such awareness of the peace and the love of God. This is the very peace and love of which I have been aware when praying with the dying. God is always available to us. Too often we fail to be aware of Him.

As well as the Holy Spirit and whole company of Heaven there are evil spirits and occult practices. Many people are tempted to contact their beloved through an occult medium. This is expressly forbidden; it is dangerous and can be devastating. Despite all the evidence, there are many who are unable to put their trust in God and there are also those who are desperately angry with God for taking away their beloved. These people need special help and there should be trained bereavement counsellors in all parishes. All bereaved people, however deep their faith, benefit from the sensitive support of friends. Many wish in the early days to be alone with family and very close friends, but letters of condolence and appreciation of the qualities of the deceased do help. Our Lord instructed His disciples that when facing trial they should not worry about what to say, the Holy Spirit would give them the words to utter. This is also appropriate for us when visiting bereaved people. Many words can be poured out in a confused torrent, which only causes embarrassment. A kiss and a hand on the shoulder say it all. Sharing the pain of loss, giving loving support, is what is needed. Be sensitive, do not stay too long and leave counselling to those who are trained.

Certain theologians, including the Reverend Dr Martin Israel, have a theory that in the space of aeons of time, even the soul of such as Hitler might be purified to heavenly state. This does give a glimmer of hope for those whose loved one might not have been considered 'eligible'. I believe the following lines express our true relationship with the departed. I have often quoted them in letters of condolence and people do find them helpful:

'Death hides, it does not divide
Thou art on Christ's other side
Thou art with Christ
And Christ with me
Through Him thou art
Still linked to me.'

'Through Him': this is our means of contact. The closer we get to the Lord in prayer, contemplation and works, the closer we are to those souls already with Him. Of course, we have many memories and photographs and it is good and helpful at times to relive the past, but not, as some people do, to get buried in it. Archbishop William Temple gave helpful guidance on prayer for the departed. Adoration of God is sharing the ways of the whole company of Heaven; pray for those we know and love who have passed on: 'We should pray for all good things because it is the Father's will to give them. We pray because we know He loves and cares for them and we claim the privilege of uniting our love for them with God's. Let us also ask them to pray for us, for our fellowship with them is in Christ and we find them only when we seek them in His name.'

If we have true faith we know that God will care for departed souls. No amount of pleading in prayer will influence this. Nevertheless, if we feel the need to remember prayerfully our departed relatives and friends, then it must be right to do so. Every Saturday evening I remember my departed family members and friends, including many killed in the War. Many of my school friends were killed within three or four years of leaving school. I was nineteen when war was declared in 1939 and it seems relevant in a chapter on death to record our feelings at the time. No sane person wants war; it is a sin to kill and one respects genuine Christian pacifists, many of whom were prepared to face danger as stretcher-bearers and medical orderlies in action. One of the most decorated officers in the First World War was a non-combatant Anglican chaplain, the Reverend Theodore Bayley Hardy VC, DSO, MC. Very sadly he died of wounds a few days before the Armistice in 1918.

We knew that Hitler was entirely evil and he was taking over countries by force of arms and enslaving them. Nearly all my friends nearing call-up age were eager to get into the fight against evil, a fight which was supported by all the churches. Those friends knew the dangers, yet such was their keenness of spirit and their longing to get into action that many were killed. 'They grow not old, as we that are left grow old. Age shall not weary them, nor the years condemn. At the going down of the sun and in the morning we will remember them.' Those moving words are spoken before the two minutes silence at the Service of Remembrance. 'Age shall not weary them,' is true, for we remember them as they were, full of life, in their teens or twenties, not old like us, as they would now be if they had survived. The message from those at the ferocious battle of Kohima is also worth recording: 'When you go home tell them of us and say: "For your tomorrows we gave our today." ' War is a time when the nation turns to God, when we acknowledge our need of Him. The volume of prayers ascending in wartime soars and many prayers certainly were answered. There have been countless incidents in war that bore the mark of divine intervention.

In the Old Testament, the Israelites were saved from the pursuing Egyptians when the Red Sea parted to allow the Israelites across and then closed in and drowned the Egyptian army. It is not even recorded that the Israelites had prayed.

God will act to further His purposes and if He has a task for someone to fulfil, He will preserve that person until his work is done. God does not always wait for prayer. By a fortunate coincidence, the day after writing this I received the *Church Times* containing the review of a book, *Almost Like A Dream: A Parish At War 1914–18* by Canon M Austin:

The relationship of these ordinary men to matters spiritual emerges through the letters. They write of attending communion services carrying their ammunition, and of a sense of divine protection in surviving the onslaughts of battle. Canon Austin senses their sincerity as they comment on how their faith upheld them through their darkest hours . . . 'Always pray for my safety, for God is my only help and defence'. When these men could not resolve difficult questions about how God could side with such slaughter, they took on trust the pronouncements of the religious authorities . . . that this was a just war.

Reconciliation is another important area where prayer concerning the departed is helpful. Any unresolved disagreements, hurts, matters needing forgiveness, misunderstandings, things left unsaid – these can be a continuing source of regret, remorse or guilt. 'If only . . .' we say; the good news is that we can. Any of these matters we can take to God in prayer and ask for them to be passed on. We can also make confession of any guilt we may feel regarding our past relationship with the departed, or hurts inflicted by us in any way. This helps to put it all behind us, as I have personally experienced, and it has been a great relief to me. If we make confession and receive absolution the matter is finished. To continue to worry is denigrating God, harming ourselves and helping no one. Confession is often regarded as something which only takes place for Roman Catholics. Although not normally mentioned in Anglican circles, to have sacramental confession is a valuable and healing experience for anyone with a sense of guilt. I am fortunate in having a spiritual director who is a revered member of a religious Order, but I have also made confession for a specific matter to the rector of a local Anglo-Catholic church. Any Anglican wishing for further information would be able to obtain it from an Anglo-Catholic church in their area.

Prayer for the dying is not always a case of asking God for further remission. Dr Gareth Tuckwell, for many years director of Burrswood Christian Centre for Healthcare and Ministry, writes about his father's death:

. . . three weeks before his death, after taking Holy Communion, he shared with his vicar: 'You know, all those prayers for my healing were answered. The depression I was going into a year ago has left me completely and so has all fear of dying; I know it won't be long now.' Nevertheless, he still struggled to stay in control in the face of the confusion of overwhelming infection. Then the family prayed at the bedside: 'Father God, take your servant to yourself; we release him from our love and ask that you release him from any suffering or indignity.' A hot hand squeezed mine in agreement and a few minutes later that prayer was answered – what might have lasted hours or days was over – the final healing had taken place. My father looked refreshed, peaceful and asleep.

If you were going on a long journey to stay with someone for the first time, it would be helpful before leaving to find out all you could about the person who is to be your host. The thought came to me that those who reach retirement age have the great advantage of time in which to develop their relationship with God by studying, going on retreats, praying and perhaps meditating – or even writing about Him! We are approaching the most important journey that any of us will ever make, yet so many make no preparations at all other than consigning their earthly baggage to their inheritors.

I am aware that to be present with people who are dying is a tremendous privilege and on these occasions I have felt a very deep peace and an awareness of the presence of God, perhaps more deeply than at any other time. Obviously no visit should be made without making sure that the family would appreciate it. Many families, quite understandably, prefer to be alone and undisturbed except for very close friends and perhaps a visit by an ordained minister. These remarks apply equally to visiting the bereaved and one must be sensitive regarding the family and any relatives or friends who may also be visiting.

Journey prayerfully, unhurried and in the peace of Christ. Recently I awoke in the early hours of the morning with a feeling of intense guilt on this score. It had been a busy day and there was more to be done, but we had received news that one of our splendid Cancer Group members, visited in hospital by Sue and I on a number of occasions, was dying and semi-conscious in a Farnham nursing home. I phoned the nursing home and got there as quickly as I could. I could not describe that as a prayerful journey and when I arrived I was told that Alvis was semi-conscious and that a niece was visiting her. I should, of course, have talked sensitively with the niece, told her that all of us who knew her aunt in the Cancer Group had such a high regard for her, she was so full of courage and humour . . . I did not follow my rules but, feeling pressed for time, I knelt by the bedside and gently put my hand on Alvis' head with a softly whispered prayer. I got back home in record time, but I awoke at 4 a.m. the next morning, with the horrendous realisation of how insensitive I had been in not showing concern for the niece. I wrote to her, Fenella, and apologised and made further amends later. This is the first time in over twenty years of visiting people who are sick and dying that I am aware of having shown discourtesy. I sincerely hope that it will be the last and I give this testimony against myself as a warning to others. Travel prayerfully and bring with you the peace of the Lord. I am happy to be able to record that Fenella, a young mother with problems of her own, is now being regularly visited at her home and she attended our Thanksgiving and Remembrance Day.

The reader may well think: 'It's all very well to pontificate about bereavement, do you know what it really feels like?' Yes, I do.

I mentioned in an earlier chapter the harmful results of resentment. It is understandable in cases such as the death of a child that there can be resentments, including resentments against God. The ensuing bitterness eats into the person and they become deeply embittered and inconsolable. Much harm results and no good can possibly come of resentment and particularly resentment against God. I have heard a number of Christians state that resentment is perfectly natural and it is not wrong to be angry with God, but I am not happy with this. I prefer the idea that one can question God: 'Oh God, why? Why? Why? We know that you are good, loving and just, but why this?' A distinguished friend of ours whose young wife was killed in the war when a German bomb struck their home and chapel, wrote: 'God has seen fit to take my darling wife, may His holy name be praised!' Not only was the chapel fully restored but one of his houses was given to the diocese and in later years our friend and his second wife established in their own home a Christian community for people in need. The community work continued elsewhere after his death and the family have continued the Christian traditions and the chapel flourishes. How different it would have been if our friend had been resentful and vented his anger on God. His was an example of true Christianity.

Through deep suffering and loss, faith can vanish or be weakened, yet it can also be wonderfully strengthened to the exclusion of all bitterness and resentments. A visitor to our Cancer Group Thanksgiving and Remembrance Day wrote afterwards: 'It was an amazing experience to witness people's faith after suffering so much, either themselves or their loved ones.'

There are many helpful passages in the New Testament on the subject of everlasting life and many of these are used in the funeral service. One of my favourites is John 3:16: 'For God so loved the world that he gave his only Son, that everyone who has faith in him may not perish but have eternal life.' These words were spoken by Jesus to Nicodemus, who was destined later to arrange the removal of the body of Jesus from the cross and its burial in his own tomb.

I find it sad that many good people with no experience of God or of the church take the attitude that they have not served God in their lives and therefore have no place in Heaven. Those who deny God's existence presumably have no eternity expectations. Matthew 19:17–24 contains the following relevant sayings of Jesus: 'But if you wish to enter into life, keep the commandments.' However, for the rich it is more difficult: 'It is easier for a camel to pass through the eye of a needle than for a rich man to enter the kingdom of God.' The rich are doing God's will if they are compassionate and helpful to those in need and with that goes the assurance of entry to His kingdom.

The significance of God's gift of peace to the dying is powerfully illustrated by two contrasting experiences. Before going to sleep one Sunday night, I read a very moving passage from George Bennett's book *The Heart of Healing*. After ministering to a young nurse, too ill with cancer to walk to the sanctuary, the Reverend George Bennett had visited her in her flat. She said:

This is the first time I have been on the receiving end of prayer and it is wonderful. I've joined in prayer with my friends for the healing of many people and I am now finding what it is like to be so blessed. I know you won't feel sorry for me because paradise seems so close and I would not have this realisation taken from me for anything that anyone could give. If only we could experience a thing like this when life is normal! What a difference it would make to the world!

By coincidence, the morning after reading this, I received a letter from the wife of an American business friend:

> This has been a heartbreaking year for us. About fifteen months ago we found out that John's daughter, Karen, had cancer of the stomach and lungs. Three months ago she moved in with us and I took a leave of absence to care for her. She is terrified of hospitals and we decided we could handle it here at home. It's an emotionally draining experience for all of us. Karen wants a lot of people round her all the time – she sleeps sitting up in the living room; she is terrified of the dark, of being alone and of a quiet house. So we keep the lights and television on twenty-four hours, the house full of company and when she is alone and afraid, I sit with her.

I wrote to Karen's family, mentioning the Christian healing ministry and my own faith. I gave assurance of my prayers and offered to fly over and talk to Karen, a bright girl in her early twenties, whom I had met on a business visit to the USA. The reply was appreciative but the offer of a visit was not accepted. I am sure that there could not be more human love and caring than Karen was receiving. Yet the contrast between Karen and the young nurse, also dying of cancer, could hardly be more striking. Both in the advanced stages of cancer, one was filled with joy and peace and the love of God, the other with terror and fear of being alone.

In hospitals and homes throughout the world there are so many people suffering without being aware of our Lord's transforming love and power. The peace of mind and freedom from fear enjoyed by a believer is a gift beyond price. We see it in the lives of our terminally ill cancer patients. It remains on offer for all who wish to claim it.

Of course, it is not only the terminally ill who face death; it can strike without warning and at any age, as we were to be reminded.

Chapter 12

CHRISTOPHER

Christopher, my grandson, then aged twelve, was very special. He had an amazing ability to communicate with young and old alike and if you were on the receiving end of Christopher's flashing smile you wouldn't ever forget it. He was a great animal lover and had a wonderful way with them – the Jersey cows, Angus his white Westie and his four ferrets: Pete, Strawberry, Pudding and Weasel. They were all a very important part of Christopher's life. Getting up at 5 a.m. to be with his beloved animals and the farm staff was not a problem and he was as adept at handling the cattle as the most experienced cowmen, always gentle but firm.

Chris was on his way to the cows at an early hour on 18th August 1997 when his clothing got caught up in the wheel of his child's motorbike and strangled him. An hour later, walking with the dogs down the same track towards the cattle, Mike, his father, spotted the cycle lying on its side; he assumed that it had broken down and that Christopher had walked on. To his horror, when he approached, Mike found Christopher unconscious, lying beside the bike. He called an ambulance and phoned me, desperately asking us to pray. A cowman gave artificial respiration but it was too late. Shortly afterwards Mike phoned again to say that Christopher was in Heaven. He asked me to phone his wife Sarah, who was out with their daughter Katrina, asking her to come at once to the hospital, but I was not to tell her that Christopher was dead. Despite being alone in these horrendous circumstances

Mike was wonderfully calm. After phoning Sarah I felt I must go at once to see Mike at the hospital, persuading Sue to remain by the phone. It would be a short visit, as I knew that Mike would want to be alone when Sarah arrived. We said little: it was not a time for words but for just being there. My next priority was confidentially to inform Nicola, secretary to Mike and myself. I knew that there would soon be rumours and it was important that Nicola, the nerve centre of the office, should be aware of the tragedy. The police were around and very soon people began to hear, then the local radio station got hold of it and the press were on the phone. On that first day, our phones were soon ringing, with people sending their condolences. Over the next week we received between us over a thousand letters, many from people assuring us of their prayers and some informing us that they were holding special services for Christopher. All these messages were enormously appreciated and a great help. We were enveloped in a great blanket of support and sympathy. A surprisingly large number mentioned that they themselves had suffered bereavement through the death of a young person, sometimes in childhood when a brother or sister had died or been killed in an accident. This formed a special bond between us.

Christopher's ashes were scattered on the farm and in the garden at places that were special to him and a Service of Thanksgiving was held at St Nicholas Church, Compton. The church was packed, with almost as many standing outside. Christopher was very special and his character comes out in the splendid address given at the funeral by his housemaster, Brother Christopher Powell OGS. We all regarded it as an outstanding address, not only in the portrayal of Christopher, but in putting a Christian perspective on the death of one so young. I could not find a single paragraph that I felt I could omit and I hope that readers will endorse my decision.

Funeral Address for Christopher James
More-Molyneux
Compton Church – Friday 22nd August 1997

In the name of the Father and of the Son and of the Holy Spirit. Amen.

We are gathered here today to give thanks to Almighty God for the life of Christopher, a young man who was to many people so many different things: a son, grandson, a brother, a friend to so many and to us all, just simply 'C'.

It is surely a tribute to what he meant to us all that in a short lifetime he had gathered around him such a group of friends that here we are today full to overflowing.

I can't help but think that he would have an enormous grin on his face if he could have seen that he had got more press coverage even than the Spice Girls! I gather from Mike and Sarah that he even hit the headlines in Australia and New Zealand!

And for me, not just a pupil but a young man, I have the privilege to think of Chris as being a friend. As I was planning what I was going to say today I couldn't help but think of him grinning at, 'What are you going to say about me then Sir?' Because he certainly wouldn't have wanted me to be either trite or patronising, but to make sure that people left this church today with hope in their hearts and a sure faith that we are saying farewell and not goodbye forever.

Telephoning people over the last few days to let them know what had happened, I lost count of the number of stories that people told me about Christopher and the constant theme was 'full of life, happy, smiling, busy, in a rush, yes always in a rush.'

In fact Sarah tells me that on the day he was born he didn't even bother to wait for his father and made a hurried appearance into the world sooner than even the hospital could cope with. We joked on his last birthday, Coronation Day, that I was flying the flag for him and not the Queen! We even, he said, provided him with champagne – only thinly disguised as Tizer!

How many of us from school have either been nearly mown down by the rollerblading Chris, by the skiing Chris or by the boy rushing to go shooting or fishing in the lake, or by the mad scamp on the rugby field.

Tidy he never was, 'Too much stuff, Sir, for this dormitory,' and that winning and disarming smile would take the wrath out of any irate house master.

How lucky for a boy of Chris' temperament that he was born into a family who lived on the land. How very wrong it would have been to try to contain his enthusiastic spirit by stopping him doing the things he wanted and loved – indeed who would have dared?

It is rare to see in anybody, let alone a child, such a love of nature, a care for animals and the outdoors and how appropriate it is that some of his artwork reflecting that love of nature adorns the back cover of our service sheet today.

How much it reflects Christopher's nature that the factor that won him over to going to Milton Abbey for his next school after Aldro was that the headmaster would allow him to keep his ferrets at school. It is strangely fitting that the accident that cut his life so tragically short would be on his way to help milk cows, and a tragic death indeed. To find comfort, real comfort, in these dark days will be something very hard indeed for all those who knew Christopher and loved him and most especially his family whom I commend to your love and prayers, for that is what they will really need in the weeks and months and even the years to come.

I know how overwhelmed they have been by the hundreds of letters they have received – many from Christopher's school chums. I know too how keen they are that their friends and Christopher's friends should still feel free to visit – there are not right or wrong things to say, just be yourselves, for that is what they really need.

Many of you, as Christopher did, will know the chapel at Aldro in which he would have said his prayers day in and day out for the years he was there as a schoolboy. Behind the altar there we have two windows: on one side the birth of our Lord Jesus and on the other His death on the cross.

In the one, the joy of His earthly family giving thanks for His birth and in the other His family and friends grieving for a life so cruelly cut short. Between them there is an image of our Lord reigning in glory from His cross. And it is to that Lord, reigning, that we turn our thoughts today, for it is only in the love of that God who sent His Son to die for us that I can make any sense at all of the events of the past week.

Later in the service we will hear familiar words of our Lord, 'I am the way, I am the truth and the life, no one can come to the Father except through me.' 'In my Father's house there are many mansions, and I am going there ahead of you to prepare a place for you.' The same God who gave us freedom of choice at the beginning of Creation, and in the words of John Milton the freedom to 'Lose the paradise he had created for us,' is surely the same God who gives us the freedom to love Him and to know Him and to follow that way which is His Son, Jesus.

He is the same God who allows us the freedom to make decisions which can in the worst circumstances lead to tragedies such as we all face today.

But He is also the same God who gives us hope in the midst of such tragedy and adversity. Are we going to be a people stuck in the misery of Good Friday or are we going to go forward in the faith that is the faith of all Christians? An empty tomb; paradise found; and eternal life.

There is a line in the liturgy for the Vigil of Easter which says, 'What good would life have been to us if Christ had not come as our redeemer?' Only a few short weeks ago Christopher had been away with some of his school friends on a Scripture Union Holiday, where one of the Leaders described Christopher's sunny nature as an outward reflection of his inner faith. On his return he made a comment about the religious input each evening, and said, 'Well it makes you think, doesn't it?' And so today makes us think.

Death will come to us all and for Christopher far, far too soon, but we must rejoice in the promise of eternal life. 'For to His faithful people life is changed, not taken away, and when this mortal flesh is laid aside an everlasting dwelling place is made ready for us in Heaven.'

Don't go from this church today just with an image of a life cut short, of the futility and waste of it all. Be happy to talk about Christopher, remember that sunniness, that happiness, that creativity, that smile, that joy in life, that enthusiasm about the beauty of nature. Don't leave him as a memory in a coffin. Don't make his name and his memory something of which to be frightened.

Anybody who thinks that Christopher could possibly be overcome by the powers of death is somebody who didn't really know him at all.

Weep and weep we must, but not for someone who is lost, but for someone very precious with whom one day we will be reunited.

For him paradise has been found a jolly sight sooner than most of us have found it and our Lord's most loving arms are now enfolding him.

To misquote Cardinal Newman, 'Farewell, but not forever dear brother.' And we must, 'Be brave and patient' until the day we are reunited with him.

In the words of St Francis' *Canticle of the Sun*, words with which Christopher was very familiar from school, 'Death, once the ancient enemy, hear now our Easter melody. O praise him, Alleluia. You are the pathway home to God, our door to life, through Christ our Lord. O praise him, Alleluia.'

I shall end with some words of Richard Baxter, a seventeenth-century priest, 'Christ leads me through no darker rooms than He went through before. He that unto God's kingdom comes must enter by this door. My knowledge of that life is small, the eye of faith is dim, but 'tis enough that Christ knows all and I shall be with Him.' Amen.

The funeral, at which this address was given, took place just four days after the accident. Mike and Sarah were prepared to give positive interviews to the press over the next few days, and these featured in the main national daily papers, the *Daily Telegraph* following up with a more detailed feature.

Only five weeks after the accident Mike was on Radio 4's *Prayer For The Day*, giving his testimony of faith:

Interviewer: My guest this morning is a farmer, someone who would have been quite content to spend his life in relative anonymity at his four-hundred-year-old family home near Guildford in Surrey where he runs the celebrated Loseley Estate. But five weeks ago a tragic domestic accident changed all that. When Michael More-Molyneux discovered his twelve-year-old son Christopher dying beside the trail bike on the farm he loved so much, both he and his family found themselves propelled into the newspaper headlines. I asked him whether at that time of anguish and loss, prayer had been a real comfort.

Mike: Prayer was a great help and assistance to Sarah and I, the death of a young member of the family is something you obviously are not trained for. It takes you completely by surprise and you have feelings which you have never experienced before. But I think also and probably more importantly, the prayer of others and we literally had thousands and do have still thousands of people praying for us and for Christopher and that is so much appreciated.

Interviewer: Now the paradox of the prayer you have chosen is that it is very much about life and not death, but I think the first line says it all 'Do not stand by my grave and weep'. Do you think that is the tone that's set?

Mike: I think so because he was very much a get-up and go boy. He was always in a rush, and yes, he had time for everybody and he wouldn't have wanted us to weep until November and to laugh with him about all the wonderful incidents and memories that we've shared. Yes, but not to weep for the sake of it. That's not to say that we are both totally composed all the time, obviously we're not. But we do have three other wonderful children and it's important for them to go forward as a family into the future.

Interviewer. Another thing that the prayer focuses on is the seasonal comfort of nature and pastoral element, that presumably is a significant factor with such beautiful surroundings as Loseley.

Mike. Well, Christopher was very much the country boy and he was very annoyed with me the morning he died because I woke him up at a quarter to six instead of half past five, and he loved getting up early, he loved his cows and he loved working with the chaps on the farm and their friendship and he loved nature, he was a brilliant skier so the line about the snowflakes was also very appropriate for Christopher.

Interviewer. It's just that the prayer itself is very much a celebration of a life rather than mourning for a death.

Mike. Absolutely, we like to think of it as Christopher being the twelve-year-old wonderful son who we had the privilege and pleasure of loving and living with for twelve wonderful years and we look forward to meeting up with him and, as one prayer said, he's just gone on ahead.

Interviewer. Because the prayer that you've chosen ends on the fundamental belief in the life everlasting where all shall be well.

Mike. Absolutely, and all will be well too:

> Do not stand by my grave and weep
> I am not there, I do not sleep

I am a thousand winds that blow
I am a diamond glint on snow
I am the sunlight on ripened grain
I am the gentle autumn rain
When you awake in the morning hush
I am the swift uplifting rush of quiet birds in
   circling flight
I am the soft star-shine at night
Do not stand by my grave and cry
I am not there, I did not die.'

Through his own experience and faith, Mike has been able to assist a number of parents who have suffered similar family bereavements and has been called upon for help by people he had never met. With their parents' lead, Mike and Sarah's children have coped wonderfully and there are further positive results. A children's hospice is to be built on our land and Mike and Sarah are playing a leading role in CHASE, the S.E. children's hospice charity. They have both completed a London marathon and Mike has done a third London as well as the New York marathon, and is booked in for New York with his eldest son, Alexander, in November 2000. He is captain of the CHASE marathon team with over £200,000 already received in sponsorship. Christopher would be thrilled and the hospice will be named after him.

Grieving is natural and necessary, under-girded with faith and love it becomes positive and bearable, but things will never be the same again. In a sense the loss of Christopher could be likened to the refining process of going through the fire of a furnace, by which we have all emerged strengthened, particularly Mike and Sarah and the children. We give thanks that even tragedy can be turned to the good of others in need and to the glory of God.

Time passes and I am now writing these final paragraphs in the third year since Chris left us. By the palm trees fringing the rose garden is a lovely memorial headstone to him, with a stone ferret on the top. Christopher's live ferrets still live in their large cage and Angus, his Westie, enjoys special attention. No question of anything occult, but there will always be the feeling of Chris still being among us as part of the family. When asked: 'How many children do you have?' Mike's answer is always: 'Four, one in Heaven'.

Mike's generation happily have not had a war to contend with and in a way this terrible bereavement has been, for him, the occasion for proving his mettle. Mike has become leaner and fitter and in addition to continuing to play a major part with Sarah in the establishment of the children's hospice and the fundraising, he runs the Loseley business, has many voluntary commitments and is always prepared to assist other bereaved families. He is High Sheriff of Surrey for the year from April 2000.

The children are all doing splendidly. Tristram, the youngest, competed in the English schools skiing championship and is captain of his school shooting team and has been awarded an art scholarship to Milton Abbey School. Encouraged by their parents' enthusiasm, they are all brilliant skiers and Katrina has achieved her Inter Gold at skating, thanks partly to Sarah's dedication in setting off regularly at 5 a.m. to collect her from school for training. Alexander, the eldest, has done well academically and on the games field and was RAF Cadet of the Year at Milton Abbey. He is captain of the school Ten Tors climbing team and was chosen for a term's exchange at Bishop's School, Cape Town.

Family achievements are unspokenly regarded as something for Christopher, which makes them special. Alexander, the eldest, has done extremely well academically, on the games field and as a RAF cadet. For his last year at school he has been appointed Head of School at Milton Abbey.

Chapter 13

PRAYER, MEDITATION AND GUIDANCE

If you ... pray to me, I shall listen to you:
When you seek me, you will find me;
if you search wholeheartedly,
I shall let you find me
Jeremiah 29:12–13

It is important to note the condition: 'If you search wholeheartedly.' I suspect that there may be others who, like me, knew little about prayer until middle age. 'God bless Mummy and Daddy', the Lord's Prayer and intercessions for the sick was about it. Prayer and meditation are vital to our relationship with God, to our Christian life and work, and to the healing ministry. I again emphasise that I am neither expert nor teacher: I merely share my experiences and what I have learned. From childhood most Christians have prayed for friends and relatives who are ill. It is the natural thing to do and I must have been praying in this way for forty years before I was aware that there was a Christian healing ministry.

Every Christian should pray for the healing of their friends – and expect it to happen. I do commend a little book by Francis McNutt, *The Prayer That Heals*. This emphasises that the most appropriate person to pray for the healing of a child is the mother of that child. I have heard personal testimonies from mothers of how they have prayed for their babe, or small child, when desperately ill and healing has taken place almost immediately.

The word 'prayer' for many people has a rather boring, dutiful flavour and long formal church prayers do not always hold one's full committed attention. They are usually prefaced by 'Let us pray.' One small boy responded: 'What a good idea!' Yes, it is and when we realise that prayer is communicating with God who loves us, prayer becomes exciting, to be anticipated with joy in our hearts. I wish I could say that this always applied to me, but sometimes it certainly does. If we love someone, we need to converse with them, listening as well as speaking and perhaps, best of all, just being silently aware of each other and of our love. This is the way that prayer should be. In serving God we need to know His will in all situations. If we ask and listen we should receive an answer, then we need to obey.

The more natural and simple and open to God that we can be, the better. We do not need know-how, complicated procedures or devout phrases to ask for God's healing. We ask in reverence, love, humility, faith and expectancy. There are many books on prayer, but Anglicans do not seem to receive much teaching on the subject in the church. If they go in search of it there is excellent teaching to be had on prayer and meditation.

When they are ill, most people, even non-believers, appreciate being told that they are being prayed for. I pass on an excellent suggestion that I was given – when you are suffering any pain or illness pray also for those who may be suffering more. Many people only pray when they need help. Others feel unable to pray in their own words and use set prayers. I can only write about my own experience and things that I have learned. Prayer is absolutely vital. If it is true communication with God it needs to be two-way and to give time to 'listen' to God. I do know people who do their praying in the train, and although one can certainly pray anywhere – especially in a hazardous situation – one's daily prayer should be in a private place. Our Lord said: 'Close the door.'

During the War I usually prayed outside at night. In a desert or on a seashore this is ideal. A quiet spot in the countryside or in a garden can also be good, as long as the weather is not too boisterous. After the War, for many years I used the bathroom for prayer, very early in the morning. Now we have the luxury of a chapel. I normally prefer prayer before breakfast, but otherwise in the evening, and a daily half-hour rule. I have lists of people to be prayed for; those who are ill or in need, and a daily programme of intercessions for bishops, priests, deacons, monks and nuns. Various Christian organisations and hospitals, hospices and homes of healing are remembered weekly. When praying for homes of healing, I pray for the staff, helpers and all who go for healing, refreshment or training, that in all things God may be glorified. I have a clear awareness that God appreciates that ending. I find that it is important to have time available in prayer for anything that comes into one's mind that should be shared with God – any immediate concerns or matters for repentance. I am not an expert and I quite often feel that I would rather be meditating than praying a long list of intercessions.

Very important, of course, are prayers for people who are very ill. These are remembered daily, often more than once in the day and in the night and early morning. All members of our Cancer Group and Parkinson's Disease Group and associates are remembered on Monday and Tuesday respectively unless on the daily list. Like many others, Sue and I pray sometimes for people in the news who are in trouble. At the time of the Russian bombardment of Chechnya, a girl dying of tuberculosis was featured on the TV and in the press. A week or so earlier, virtually without food, she had watched her mother dying of tuberculosis while they sheltered from the bombardment in a cellar.

Surely millions must have prayed for this girl. There are so many wars, natural disasters and accidents. It is certainly appropriate to offer prayers for all involved and for the bereaved and there is always a real need for prayers for peace.

A few minutes being 'open' to God in meditation is something I regard as a great blessing, one might almost say a luxury. Anyone who has a problem with meditating should be encouraged to seek instruction: it is simple and most people find it helpful in coming closer to God.

God does not always answer our questions or our prayers while we are meditating, but those who meditate do find that answers, which clearly are from God, suddenly come into the mind at a later time, in the form of guidance or discernment. We badly need these and unless we pray and come close to God, we cannot expect Him to guide us and the closer we come to God the more we can be aware of His will.

One of my fellow founder members of Acorn Christian Healing Trust, Mrs Anna Evans, teaches meditation, in words that you and I can understand. I have Anna's permission to quote a few passages from one of her lectures:

> Meditation, sometimes called the prayer of the heart, brings us into a place of silence before God. As we praise Him so our love for Him is awakened and our spirit responds to His Holy Spirit within us. Then we need to be silent before Him, and allow His Spirit to speak to us, and to change us more and more into the person He wants us to be, always growing in love for Him. In meditation we stop our chatter and our noise, we stop looking at our own needs and desires and concerns, and remain simply in God's presence. Our intercession becomes more and more guided by the Holy Spirit. As St Paul says: 'We do not know how to pray, but the Holy Spirit prays in us.'

The prayer of praise moves on to the prayer of thanksgiving and from there to the silence of meditation, leading into intercession for the needs of the world. There is a lovely story about an old French peasant, who used to go every day into the village church and just sit there looking at the altar. One day the priest, who had noticed the old man for some time, asked him what he was doing just sitting there day after day. 'Well,' said the peasant, 'it's like this: I looks at Him and He looks at me.' That is really what meditation is all about. God wants our friendship. Jesus told his disciples: 'You are my friends.' He also said: 'Dwell in my love. If you heed my commands you will dwell in my love, as I have heeded my Father's commands and dwell in His love.' The peasant was dwelling in the Father's love.

From time to time we read that Jesus spent all night alone in prayer, going up into the hills above Galilee.

O Sabbath rest by Galilee,
O calm of hills above,
Where Jesus knelt to share with Thee
The silence of eternity
Interpreted by love.

It was in these times of silent communion that Jesus sought His Father's will.

St Paul must have spent long hours with God in silent meditation to be able to say with such confidence: 'I speak God's hidden wisdom.' In the third century AD, Anthony, a young Christian Egyptian, feeling in danger of being overwhelmed by the cares of the world and temptations of city life, fled into the desert where he lived for many years a life of prayer and relying only on Jesus Christ for help. He surrendered himself completely to God. When he returned to the city, people recognised in him a wisdom, love and wholeness and he was sought as a counsellor and spiritual advisor. Others followed and went into the desert to find silence and solitude, to grow closer to God and a monastic life was begun.

Since then down the ages men and women have left everything to find God in silence, either in community, or, more rarely, in the complete solitude of the life of the hermit.

Meditation is about being still with God, letting Him speak to us and being attentive to Him. Some people find it helpful to look at a candle or some other object to focus attention. Alternatively we can use words. St John's Gospel is full of symbols – Jesus the light of the world, Jesus the true vine, the good shepherd, living water . . . Any of these can be used as a focus for meditation. A symbol I have found helpful was an open window, signifying the breath of the Holy Spirit. One can use a phrase or a single word and repeat it slowly, savouring it, not thinking about it too much, but allowing it to speak to the heart. Examples – Be still and know that I am God; Come, Lord Jesus; Christ whose glory fills the skies; Christ the True, the only light. Or, just Jesus; Glory; Abba; Father.

Another way of practising meditation is to take a passage from the Gospels and read it very slowly, a phrase at a time, listening to what God is saying in the passage. Stay with any phrase that holds your attention and use it as you do with the phrases above. Let it hold the attention and speak to the heart. This is a good way of praying the Lord's Prayer which all too often we rush through.

When St Catherine of Sienna was at prayer, she heard the Lord say to her: 'Empty the cup and I will fill it.' This is what He will ask of anyone who persists in prayer.

The foregoing are short extracts from Anna's paper on prayer and meditation. One final gem: 'To pray without awareness of God's presence is like trying to sew without first threading the needle.' For anyone wishing to study further this important subject, there are many books and short courses available.

I personally consider that simplicity is very important in religion and we should avoid the technicalities as much as possible. There need be nothing high-tech about our communication with God. None of us can claim to be as close to God as was St Paul, nearly two thousand years ago or St Anthony in the desert less than three centuries later. They did have the advantage of a quieter, slower-moving environment but their God is our God and we have the advantage of their experience and teaching. Even in those days St Anthony found it necessary to find solitude in the desert!

With such emphasis on prayer, are we coming away from the healing ministry? On the contrary. Our Lord, whose healing ministry we attempt to follow, spent nights in prayer, as did St Paul, who so effectively continued that ministry. All the apostles, saints and martyrs were people of prayer, otherwise they could not have been so close to God. With any friendship, what we do counts more than what we say, but one could not imagine a close friendship without conversation. Yet there are many people who never consider conversing with God. In conversation, if we fail to listen to what our friend is trying to tell us and are only interested in asking favours, the friendship is unlikely to endure. Fortunately, God shows more patience with us than might our fellow human beings, but the more we listen, the more we hear. Until now we have been considering our own private prayers and meditation. There are, of course, a number of other forms of prayer. There are the formal prayers from a prayer book, including The Lord's Prayer, which also has its place in our own private prayers. We say this prayer so frequently that there is a danger of it becoming mechanical. Father Ignatius OFM, of Chilworth Friary, gave me a meaningful piece on the significance of this prayer, reproduced below, in abbreviated form:

Our Father which art in heaven:
We are children of God by grace
Hallowed be thy name. Thy will be done on earth as it is in heaven:
We must hallow God's name in prayer; do God's will in all things
Give us this day our daily bread:
There is no need for anxiety
Forgive us our trespasses:
God forgives us and heals our guilt when we ask Him
As we forgive those who trespass against us:
So we are gradually healed of our spirit of resentment
Lead us not into temptation but deliver us from evil:
We pray to be delivered from our personal weaknesses

Practical suggestion: This wonderful prayer has a healing power. We must persevere in it, because genuine healing takes time.

One of my favourites, which I use in my own prayer time, acknowledges in simple words the whole company of Heaven and glorifies God and His whole creation:

With angels and archangels
And with all the Company of Heaven
We laud and magnify thy glorious name
Ever praising Thee and saying
Holy, holy, holy Lord God of hosts
Heaven and earth are full of thy glory
Glory be to Thee O Lord most high.

God does need to be glorified 'to draw all men to Him'. We need to remember the angels, archangels and the whole company of Heaven, which includes all the saints and martyrs. It is right that we should acknowledge and ascribe to God the beauty of the earth. Prayers of thanksgiving are, one suspects, less frequent than prayers of petition but equally important and rewarding.

Charismatic prayer entails praying aloud in the presence of others. These prayers may be for the healing of a sick person, for peace for someone who is dying, or other intercessions. There will also be prayers of praise and thanksgiving and the singing of hymns at a charismatic prayer meeting. I discovered this form of prayer at the charismatic Prayer Group meeting that I attended in 1976, hosted and led by Bronwen, formerly Countess of Astor. Like many people, I have never found it easy to pray aloud in the presence of others and I usually feel strongly led to pray silently. If one prays aloud with others present, even if prompted by the Holy Spirit, one needs to remain aware of the other people present, listening carefully to avoid praying something that others have already prayed.

Many people do have the gift for charismatic prayer; others are led to silent prayer. In praying over a sick or dying person with just the family or friends present and perhaps one other person ministering, I normally pray softly and feel quite comfortable with this. It is right that the family should be aware of what is being prayed and, even more important, to whom one is praying. Visiting someone alone in hospital, who is near to death and unable to speak, I would normally feel led to lay a hand on their head and whisper a short prayer, mentioning peace.

One of the gifts of the Spirit, first given on the day of Pentecost, not many days after our Lord's ascension, is the gift of tongues. Some people on occasion pray in tongues. Usually, no one present in a small gathering, including the person praying, knows the meaning of the words, but they are from God. Sometimes at a large gathering some prophecy is given in tongues and another person with the gift of interpretation of tongues, interprets. I have witnessed this in a large crowd at Central Hall, Westminster. I also know of a case where someone prayed for a person in need. The person who was prayed over happened to have a knowledge of Mandarin Chinese and had been prayed for perfectly in that language. The person praying had no idea what language he was praying in and was completely ignorant of Chinese. There are many similar testimonies and there is no doubt whatever but that this is a genuine gift of the Spirit, given ever since the day of Pentecost to a limited number of Christians and to be used humbly in God's service. It is not a status symbol and damage is done by those who consider it as such and who look down on those who do not possess this gift.

We have considered the importance of prayer and meditation in developing our relationship with God and obtaining His guidance. We have free will, but God has plans for individuals and if we truly seek His will in prayer and openness to Him we receive guidance and strength. On many occasions I feel that I have been guided by God, sometimes when praying and seeking guidance and at other times when I needed to be guided but did not realise it. On a few occasions, I have prayed and then felt it right to open the Bible and let my eye alight on a passage. This is not something to be done frequently and in my case it has seemed right only two or three times a year and, on each occasion, I only opened the Bible once. I cannot emphasise sufficiently that the Holy Bible must always be treated with reverence and never used for any unseemly purpose. I would only seek guidance from it prayerfully and reverently in order to confirm God's will. I am aware of cases of misuse including a dictionary of biblical phrases for use in business letters. I once received one of these letters on a business matter and commended the sender on his biblical knowledge, but was saddened to learn that he was not a practising Christian and only treated the Bible light-heartedly. Since writing this I have, on one occasion, failed to follow the rules and suffered for it, as reported in a later chapter.

On two separate occasions I sought guidance from opening the Bible to know if I should fast for a period. On one occasion I was given our Lord's temptation in the wilderness: 'He ate nothing' and the other time produced our Lord's rules for fasting. On these two occasions I was in the chapel and opened the chapel Bible; both times I alighted first time on the relevant verse. Surely this was more than coincidence.

On another occasion I needed to know whether or not to pray for the recovery of someone who was very ill and whose parents I had to visit. In these cases, if death is inevitable, it is important not to buoy up the hopes but if a healing is in any way a possibility, then one should pray for healing and try and sustain the faith of the family. In this case, on opening the Bible my eye alighted on: 'Through Adam came death, but in Christ are all made alive.'

At another time I needed to know whether it was right to arrange for the unveiling of the picture 'The Living Christ', as one person had cast doubts on it. On this occasion, on opening the Bible my eye immediately alighted on: 'What is covered shall be uncovered' and so we went ahead with the unveiling.

At 4 a.m. one morning in County Durham, I was pondering whether or not we should purchase a factory in the north-east for Guildway. I turned to the Gideon Bible by my bedside, opened it at random and my eye fell on the Wisdom of Solomon and the woman who said: 'Cut the baby in half and divide it between us.' To me that clearly meant that we should not start another factory and split the company in half. As events proved that almost certainly would have 'killed' us.

On 31st January 2000 I was troubled by a letter which I had received from a Christian organisation, containing a false allegation. I prayed and got the clear impression that I should burn the letter. I felt that this might be unwise, as the matter should be sorted out. It was 5 a.m. but I decided to get a Bible, open it and if there was mention of burning on the page I would burn the letter. The book opened at Ezekiel 10, and the first verse on the page, verse 7: '. . . and one of the cherubim reached out to the fire that was in their midst.' So I burned the letter and from that moment my anger evaporated and I felt completely at peace.

I have on a number of occasions received divine guidance on business matters. On a Guildway contract for four hundred houses in Iran we had many problems with our clients, the Construction Bank of Iran. I had to go out and negotiate a settlement. We had a meeting with the managing director and he impressed on us that he was under government pressure not to pay any significant sum in compensation. He would meet us again next morning and he would tell us the maximum he was prepared to pay and we must state the minimum we would accept. Our manager asked me what my figure was. I am not a 'figures' man at all. I said I didn't know but that I would know when we sat down next day. I felt completely relaxed and just left it in God's hands. When we met next morning I said: '£140,000.' The MD cranked his calculating machine to convert from rials to sterling and said: '£140,400: I'll give you the extra £400!' From then on the contract ran extremely smoothly. Despite the Shah being deposed before completion, we got the bonds back from the Ayatollah's administration.

There was another, relatively minor matter for guidance.

I had very much on my mind the need to see a church member, to apologise for my comment at a meeting. The family had moved from the parish and I did not know their address but it was the sort of thing easier done face to face than by writing or telephoning. I decided to go one Saturday morning but I found that my car had a puncture. Instead of feeling frustrated, I felt complete peace and knew that somehow this was going to lead me to the person that I needed to meet. I changed the wheel and drove to Godalming Tyre Services, particularly conscious of the need to meet my friend. As I came to a junction, there was his car, going towards Godalming. I tucked myself in behind and we met in a lay-by and amicably cleared our problem. Although I had known him for many years, this was the first time I had ever found myself driving behind him. The odds against such a coincidence must be great and why should I have been aware beforehand that this would happen? Guidance, surely.

Discernment is relevant to healing in a number of contexts. A lady recently told me that her husband had died of cancer but they had had discernment to pray for absence of pain, they did this and at no time during the illness did he have any pain at all. They went away on holiday and another couple in the hotel, not knowing that he had cancer, remarked how happy the couple always looked and asked for their secret! Apart from complete healing and freedom from pain, benefits received through prayer can include reduction in side-effects of treatment and freedom from worry, which often has significant effects on health and well-being.

In our service to God it is clearly important that we should know His will and if we ask Him we must be prepared to listen for the answer and then to obey. All through both the Old Testament and the New, there are many cases of people being guided, seeing visions, dreaming dreams, or being told things by angels and these things

continue to happen today, through the power of the Holy
Spirit. Too often we are too busy to be aware of them. God
will guide us in accordance with His will and if we are intent
in following our own will then we are unlikely to be aware
of His guidance.

A few days after writing the above, I attended an Alpha
course evening at which a leaflet was issued on *How Does
God Guide Us?* One of the examples is so striking that I
include, with permission, an abbreviated version below:

Michael Bordeaux is head of Keston College, a research
unit devoted to helping believers in what were
communist lands. He studied Russian at Oxford and
his Russian teacher, Dr Zernov, sent him a letter.
Monks were being beaten up by the KGB and
subjected to inhuman medical examinations; they were
being rounded up in lorries and dumped many
hundreds of miles away. The letter was written very
simply, with no adornment, and as he read it Michael
Bordeaux felt he was hearing the true voice of the
persecuted church. The letter was signed Varavva and
Pronina.

In August 1964 he went to Moscow and on his first
evening met old friends who detailed the worsening
persecutions, in particular the old Church of St Peter
and St Paul had been demolished. They suggested that
he go and see it for himself. So he took a taxi, arriving
at dusk. When he came to the square where he had
remembered a very beautiful church, he found nothing
except a twelve-foot high fence which hid the rubble
where the church had been. Over on the other side of
the square, climbing the fence to try to see what was
inside, there were two women. He watched them and
when they left the square he followed them and
eventually caught up. They asked: 'Who are you?' He

replied: 'I am a foreigner. I have come to find out what is happening here in the Soviet Union.'

They took him back to the house of another woman, who asked him why he had come. He said he had received a letter from the Ukraine via Paris. When she asked who it was from, he replied: 'Varavva and Pronina.' There was silence. He wondered if he had said something wrong. There followed a flood of uncontrolled sobbing. The woman pointed and said: 'This is Varavva and this is Pronina.'

The population of Russia is over 140 million. The Ukraine, from where the letter was written, is 1,300 kilometres from Moscow. Michael Bordeaux had flown from England six months after the letter had been written. They would not have met had either party arrived at the demolished church an hour earlier or an hour later. That was one of the ways God called Michael Bordeaux to set up his life's work.

Surely no one could call that coincidence.

Sometimes we hear God correctly, but we get the timing wrong. God spoke to Joseph in a dream about what would happen to him and his family. He probably expected immediate fulfilment, but he had to wait years. While he was in prison it must have been hard for him to believe that his dreams would ever be fulfilled. But thirteen years after the original dream, he saw God's fulfilment. The waiting was part of the preparation (see Genesis 37–50).

We also need to be alert to receive the discernment for which we have prayed. The following is an almost unbelievable example of how an obvious sign can be overlooked. Many years ago, much to my surprise, I was asked by the Lord Lieutenant of the County to become Vice Lord Lieutenant, deputising for him when he was unavailable. It was a position that many would covet, but being shy socially I had never had ambitions in this direction. I was asked to visit the Lord Lieutenant to discuss the matter and I naturally prayed for guidance. On the way, I called to see the nun whom I sometimes consulted on spiritual matters, but unfortunately she was out. The Lord Lieutenant welcomed me at the door. I tripped on the mat and literally fell headlong at his feet on the large doormat. I should have realised that falling flat on my face was clear guidance against taking on the position, but I was too filled with embarrassment at that moment to be aware of guidance and my mind was fully occupied with arguing my unsuitability for the position. With some misgivings I eventually agreed but forcibly made the point that I would never be prepared to accept further advancement. I mention this episode to show how important it is to be alert for the answer if one has prayed for guidance. Fortunately, the answer does not usually come in such a dramatic form but usually a clear awareness of the right course comes into the mind. God's ways are unpredictable and one must be alert.

Over guidance, we all make mistakes. Sometimes, like Abraham, we try to fulfil God's plans by our own wrong methods. Like Joseph we get the timing wrong. Sometimes we feel we have made too much of a mess of our lives for God to do anything with us. But God is able to make something good out of the remainder of our lives if we will offer what we have to Him and co-operate with His Spirit. Paul writes that: 'In everything, as we know, he co-operates for good with those who love God and are called according to his purpose' (Romans 8:28).

What about us, when our prayers for healing are not answered as we hope? In every case, I believe that if we accept 'Thy will be done' and know that all will be well, even though we have not had the hoped-for response, then our relationship with God becomes strengthened.

The Father who gives his child everything asked for soon

finds that he has a spoilt child, who becomes increasingly dependent and demanding. Jesus Himself was constantly praying to the Father, and He instructed His followers to pray for their needs. He also taught that we should shut the door, for privacy, when we are praying in a room. Many blessings are given every day in response to prayer; besides miraculous healings, people receive such blessings as freedom from pain or side-effects, courage, patience. Next to the love of God, one of the greatest blessings that we can receive is the peace of God, as I discovered in November 1999. Several years before this I had broadcast for BBC Radio 4 *Prayer For The Day* on 'the peace of God which passeth understanding' and I had had a very special dream about that peace long ago, but the reality of the depth of this experience surpassed all expectations. I had not actually prayed to receive either the love of God or the peace of God, each was a very precious gift.

It must be God's prerogative to ignore prayers that are not in our own best interests in some way that He understands and that we do not. It is for our benefit that these prayers are not answered. If we remain open to God He may well reveal the reason. An obvious example is praying for the survival of a patient, where this would involve pain and frustration for the patient and continuing distress and worry for the family. In such cases, where there is doubt about the advisability of survival, it is appropriate to pray: 'Thy will be done.' In faith we know that God's will is best.

The outstanding example of prayers for healing not being answered as hoped for is no less than St Paul, who literally gave his life in the service of God. In 2 Corinthians 12:7–10, we read:

To keep me from being unduly elated . . . I was given a thorn in my flesh, a messenger of Satan sent to buffet me; this was to save me from being unduly elated. Three times I begged the Lord to rid me of it, but his answer was: 'My grace is all you need, power is most fully seen in weakness.' I am therefore happy to boast of my weaknesses, because then the power of Christ will rest upon me . . . for when I am weak, then I am strong.

Paul is not more specific about the nature of his 'thorn' but it clearly was unpleasant and his plea for healing was three times rejected.

Christians must expect to be asked why prayers are not answered and we need to be ready. If God answered all prayers, He would be Aladdin, not God. There would be no test of faith, for God would be a certainty.

If we continue to have faith when our prayers are not answered, then we shall find that our faith is strengthened. In some cases God could well be justified in taking this step in order to develop our faith.

It must happen on occasion that someone else's prayer is for an outcome contrary to that of our own prayer. To illustrate the point, the manager of a football club might pray for a win. If the opposing manager prayed likewise, presumably the result would be a draw. This is not a prayer that God should be expected to answer. The side that play most effectively will win. Any praying should come long before, such as: 'Lord give me discernment on the choice of this player; give me wisdom to make the right decision on . . .' It must be appropriate to pray that we may be guided and strengthened but not to pray for favours. In my business days I regularly prayed for strength and discernment and it was my experience of having these prayers answered at a time of deep business crisis that led to my giving my first public testimony of faith and led in turn to my first deep experience of God.

The circumstances in which prayers are made and the

expectation and faith of the person praying must be taken into account. I know that often 'arrow prayers', 'Lord help me!', at times of sudden danger or crisis are answered. At the other end of the scale, when the outcome of prayer is desperately important, some people fast and pray and hold night-long prayer vigils. On one occasion the disciples were unable to drive out an evil spirit which possessed and tormented a man's son. The father then approached Jesus and He did drive it out. The disciples afterwards asked Him why they had failed and Jesus answered: 'This kind cannot be driven out except by prayer.' This presumably meant deep prayer and not merely: 'We command you to come out in the name of the Lord Jesus.' Obviously Jesus would have greater authority over evil spirits than the disciples, and equally the disciples would have had greater authority than us.

Often we pray for the wrong thing. Either there will be no response to the prayer or it is answered in a more beneficial way. Very recently I read of another and very significant reason why prayers are sometimes not answered. The Reverend John Stott is President of the London Institute for Contemporary Christianity and a well-known writer, preacher and religious thinker. He writes in *The Deafness of God*: 'God is the champion of the poor. There are two verses in the book of Proverbs which make this clear. I only discovered them comparatively recently and they seem to me to be two of the most neglected texts in the whole of Scripture.' The first is Proverbs 21:13: 'Whoever stops his ears at the cry of the helpless will himself cry for help and not be answered.' This solemn statement should challenge us to revise our understanding of the conditions of answered prayer. If we do not listen to the poor, God says He will not listen to us. If we are deaf to their cries, He will be deaf to ours.

The writer also quotes the verse in Proverbs 29:7: 'The

righteous are concerned for the claims of the helpless, but the wicked cannot understand such concern.' This text is even more challenging. It obliges us to revise not only our understanding of answered prayer but also our definitions of righteousness and wickedness. 'If we neglect the poor, God himself will leave our prayers unanswered and will even count us among the wicked. These are serious realities to which we should pay careful attention.'

Clearly if our prayers are to be answered we must be in communion with God and not in a state of sin. I am certain that the more we pray and listen, the more we become aware of God's will for us and the closer we grow to Him. Even monks, who give their whole lives to God, have the need of spiritual directors. One does not need to be a monk or a nun to seek advice and those who feel the need to develop their prayer lives might pray to be led to the right person for help.

About two weeks after completing this chapter I was spending two days at Burrswood, working on the book. I had come for two nights but on the second day I phoned Sue and told her that I needed another day and she willingly agreed to postpone our planned visit to Hampshire to the following day. A visit to Burrswood is always a time of spiritual refreshment and, in addition to attending the Eucharist, I spent time also in the Shepherd's Hut Chapel and in Dorothy Kerin's little private chapel. After putting my things in the car, it was in this chapel that I spent my last few minutes before setting out on the journey home. I was immersed in a profound peace that signifies the presence of God. Just to be present is enough; a few words of silent prayer, adoration and thanksgiving. I felt a sudden heat and then the unmistakable feeling that I should delay my return home and attend the weekly Burrswood healing service at 11.30 a.m. It would not be over until about 1 p.m. and I would not be home until around 3 p.m. Sue and I were due to leave for our postponed visit to Hampshire in the morning. I had already let her down by postponing one day. Perhaps it was not God speaking to me but my own will. Once again, I decided that this was a case for seeking confirmation from the Bible. I was very much at fault, because before opening the book I did not follow my rule and pray to God to show me His will. I was so anxious to find a let-out that I just had in my mind: 'I do hope it does not say "stay".' It did not, but this was of no help because I had not asked to be shown His will, but had merely pushed my own will. Nevertheless, with slight relief I drove off. I became more and more depressed with every mile and soon I decided that I must phone Sue. There was no phone in sight. Eventually I saw a small Nursery Garden, where a lady kindly lent me her mobile. Sue, of course, was as understanding as always and I drove back to Burrswood. 'Thought you had gone' one of the other guests remarked when I returned. I told her my tale of shame and joined the congregation for the healing service.

I include this inglorious episode for two reasons. First, because it illustrates the importance of being completely open, particularly open to God. 'He is not mocked.' He knows us better than we know ourselves. If we need His guidance we must pray for it and be open to receive it and not try to short-circuit or manipulate it. The second reason is that, although my only purpose in writing this book is to encourage others to find the love and power of God and to glorify Him, there may be some who suspect that I consider myself in some way superior. I am an ordinary weak human being and I am often wrong.

I put down my pencil, believing that I had finished this chapter but then I became aware of loud 'birdsong' in my ears. Sometimes, in chapel or when praying, I hear either birdsong, like the 'dawn chorus', or sometimes a rustling of angels' wings. It is a strange phenomenon but coming at this moment it encourages me to feel that it is a sign of forgiveness.

P.S. A few weeks later I happened to read in Ezekiel 10:4,5 '. . . the radiance of the glory of the LORD filled the court. The sound of the wings of the cherubim could be heard as far as the outer court; it was as if God Almighty were speaking.' I am not aware of ever having read or heard these lines before. I am not suggesting that it was cherubim's wings that I heard, but for a long time I have thought of that sound, when close to God in contemplation, as angels' wings. It is good to know that I am not alone in this.

Chapter 14

HEALING OUR RELATIONSHIP
WITH CREATION

Almost universally these days creation is referred to as 'the environment'. Whatever we call it there can be no disagreement about the fact that we have made an awful mess of it, but I believe that it is more serious to be mucking-up God's creation than our environment. Likewise, it is more satisfying for the Christian to be working for God than for enlightened self-interest, though that is a by-product. St Francis, most appropriately, is now patron saint of the environment. He refers to 'Mother Earth, Brother Sun, Sister Moon, Brother Fire, Brother Wolf . . .' Why did he love the birds and beasts? Because, above all else, Francis had a burning love for God, so great that he prayed he might share the suffering of our Lord's passion. That prayer was most gloriously answered and Francis experienced the bitter agony of the cross and after that the joy and the glory. For the remainder of his life he carried on his hands, his feet and his sides the glorious marks of our Lord's suffering, the stigmata. So St Francis certainly did find union with God and he was also in union with the whole of creation. If, like St Francis, we could all be brought to the realisation that creation is sacred, we should reverence it and not destroy it. Love is a more positive motivation than fear; love is a healing ingredient, fear a barrier.

The more we become aware of our wholeness, the easier it is to align ourselves with God's purpose. As we progress on our spiritual journey, we are given new direction, new priorities and new tasks. Whatever our career, whatever our calling and circumstances, we have the opportunity of growing in harmony with God, working to His glory and of furthering the work of His creation. It is a challenging thought that we are directly involved in the work of creation, continuing God's work for better or for worse: for better if we plant, for worse if we destroy.

We have been so hell-bent on progress that we have been blind to its damaging effects. We lack humility and should be patient. The more 'advanced' our discoveries, the greater the potential dangers – nuclear energy being an obvious case. The arrival of DDT was welcomed with universal acclaim and I can well remember, in Palestine in wartime, our enthusiasm as swarms of flies dropped dead from the sides of the tent as we sprayed. No one had considered what happened next. The birds that ate the flies . . . Rachael Carson's 'The Silent Spring' tells the terrible tale of the chain of death. This is just one dramatic example but there are innumerable others of the horrendous results of mankind being too clever.

Some serious problems, such as breaching the ozone layer, are probably irreparable and cause various serious side-effects, including rising sea levels. The destruction of millions of trees by acid rain has been caused by coal-burning power stations and industrial plants. This is much more than matched by the felling of forests for timber without replanting and, worse still, the wanton destruction of rainforests, too often through ignorance and in order to provide land for cropping, for which the forest soil is quite unsuitable. Oceans are being poisoned by dumping, pumping or otherwise discharging oil, sewerage, industrial and sometimes nuclear waste. The Russian Aral Sea is the worst example. Poor fish, they have more than over-fishing to worry about. Some action is being taken to remedy these matters, but not soon enough and these things are not easy to control.

Individuals feel helpless in these situations. The two underlying causes of the problems are greed and arrogance. What can we do? We can make known our concern, we can support initiatives to improve the situation and we can use the word 'creation'. Also we should accept that we are stewards of God's creation. There are organisations such as Greenpeace, whose members care passionately. Some are even prepared to risk their lives in opposing environmentally hostile action, such as the dumping of toxic or nuclear waste at sea. I support them and admire them but only while they are not in defiance of the law. In such cases it is permissible to protect but not to use violence. I believe that this would also be the Christian view.

A wise old priest said to me when we were discussing the dangers of cloning: 'We are at the stage of Adam and Eve and the forbidden fruit in the Garden of Eden. We are in danger of being turned out. There are certain things, including the creation of life, that are the sole prerogative of Almighty God. Man, in his arrogance, is on the point of challenging this.' Even before we get turned out of Eden, the chances are that unless we become more aware of our responsibilities we shall destroy ourselves. We continue to develop ever more devastating weaponry and there are stocks of nuclear weapons in unstable areas of the world, including Russia. Saddam Hussein is developing arsenals of nerve gases, anthrax and we know not what else besides; UN inspectors are banned. It is right that we should be aware of the situation. At the present time we in the West seem obsessed with the strength of our economy and the wealth of individuals, an increasing number of whom earn more than £1 million per annum while hundreds of millions in the world are desperately poor. We are putting far too high a priority on personal wealth and 'lifestyle' and showing too little concern for protecting our environment and for the half of the earth's population who are suffering in poverty.

Today Christ stands at our door and knocks in the person of His poor. It is to Him that we open when we give aid, when we give ourselves to those in need, for He tells us plainly: 'anything you did for one of my brothers here, however insignificant, you did for me' (Matthew 25:40). We may not be able to get personally involved in limiting research in no go areas or in controlling the likes of Saddam Hussein but there is plenty that we can do to help in protecting creation nearer home and in reducing cruelty.

A less serious problem, but another aspect of our selfish disregard for our environment is litter. Few people can be aware of a beauty spot that has not been marred by dumped mattresses, sofas, fridges, junk of all sorts, cans, packets, bottles, papers and perhaps a burnt-out car. Recycling of all forms of waste is now far advanced in some countries and needs to make faster progress here – one area of technology that is entirely beneficial for creation.

The generation of electricity is a key area in the welfare of our planet. We have seen that coal-fired stations produce acid rain but this can be eliminated or very significantly reduced by filtration in the chimneys. Although expensive this must be done. The coal is available, vast sums have been expended in mechanisation in the pits, bringing higher productivity and better working conditions and there are ex-miners in mining villages needing employment. I find it strange that modern well-equipped coal mines are being shut while the Government is paying a subsidy to farmers to encourage them to grow crops of biomass, short duration willow and similar coppice for harvesting every few years as fuel for power stations. When I was a part-time board member of an Electricity Board I was given a tie bearing the slogan 'Dark Ages no thanks. Atoms for energy'. I have not worn it since Chernobyl. I now consider that the risks of nuclear power, which include the problem of dealing with spent fuel, are too great. Considerable work is being done in finding alternative means of generating power. These include wind turbines and harnessing the tides.

A few years ago a Christian inventor wrote to me about his novel new fuel:

> The process, which is fully patented, involves the use of electrical potential to crack tap water into its key constituent gases of hydrogen and oxygen – the perfect fuel . . . the original idea was inspired by Job chapter 38:22–23 amongst other references. A car is currently being equipped with a WFC hydrogen injector computer system that runs the car efficiently on water.

This is a reminder that there are more gifts from the Creator still to be unwrapped by mankind. Into my mind comes the saying: 'Enough for everyone's need but not for everyone's greed.' We are so wasteful and extravagant and this is surely not God's will.

There is too much cruelty to animals, through ignorance, profit motives or sadism. Any RSPCA inspector could cite examples to make any sound individual weep. I do not include fox hunting, for foxes do have to be controlled and none of the alternative methods is reliably less cruel. For those who really do care about animal welfare, there are many greater priorities crying out for their support, not least the banning of live export of animals for slaughter. CIWF (Compassion In World Farming) based in Petersfield, Hampshire and ILPH (Protection of Horses) for example.

The Brooke Hospital for Animals, 2, Panton Street, London SW 11 4 DR does splendid work in setting up clinics and looking after sick and ill-treated horses and donkeys and other overworked beasts of burden in India and the Middle East. Having tried to put fox hunting in perspective, if, thinking as a Franciscan, you regard the fox as a brother, it is a bit dodgy to get sport out of hunting him! Savouring my new relationship, I experienced great satisfaction in having Brother Fox come to within fifteen yards of me in a wood; he paused to look at me and went on quite unafraid. I have had similar experiences with deer in the wood. In a TV interview, which took place outside on a rustic seat, I found myself saying that the sparrow which had been sitting on the back of the seat a few minutes earlier had just as much right there as I had!

We also need to think about the production of our food – farming, gardening, the soil and our livestock. For fifty years or more there have been warnings, from people with vision, about the use of poison sprays and other chemicals in agriculture. The horrendous case of DDT has already been mentioned. Over the past twenty years there has been an increasing awareness of the dangers and of the side-effects of various agricultural and horticultural sprays and dusts. Medical practitioners such as Dr Jean Munro have been able to prove that people are dying and large numbers suffering serious ill-health as a result of allergies to various chemical substances, not necessarily poisonous, taken up through food. There are now a number of specialist allergy clinics. If we use natural manures and pest controls there is never any problem with allergies. The number of sprays and other substances to which a lettuce is subject during its short life on an intensive market garden is unbelievably large. Organic farmers, laughed at for years as 'muck and moonshine cranks', have now been proved right and the demand for organic produce of all types is exceeding demand.

The fundamental principle in organic farming is to work with nature rather than fighting against it. Harmony in accordance with the principle of St Francis. The 'chemical' farmer does not bind himself to following the rules of good husbandry, such as crop rotations – he relies on chemicals to get him out of trouble. There are special sprays to kill all known weeds without damaging the crop, others to kill most crop pests, poison pellets for slugs – one reason for the disappearance of many of our songbirds – mercury seed dressings and further powders to ward off mildew. Then there are growth inhibitors to allow for heavier dressings of artificial nitrogen without causing the straw to 'lodge'. One effective herbicide, Roundup, is often applied about two weeks before harvest to kill off the weeds under the corn to give a clean crop the following year. Inevitably some of the grain in the standing crop is contaminated. I am not at present aware of any reported ill effects attributable to bread containing flour from wheat sprayed with Roundup, but it is possible that one day problems will emerge.

At the time of writing, controversy rages on the subject of genetically modified (GM) foods and because of the very determined opposition by those organisations and individuals aware of the serious potential dangers, our nation has been rescued at the brink from once again being rushed into the unknown.

Those of us who gain our living from the land are privileged to be stewards of a part of God's creation. We have responsibility for the well-being of the permanent raw material – the soil – and for livestock, crops and woodlands. The soil itself is full of life – one gram contains 400 million micro-organisms as well as earthworms and other useful soil dwelling creatures. Soil responds to tender loving care, but these days it is more likely to get polluted, sprayed and dusted with a vast array of poison chemicals, and panned, compacted and torn apart by increasingly heavy and powerful tractors and cultivation machinery. The soil is exploited for short-term gain, the farmer being pressurised into following the advice of his computer to maximise profitability rather than obey the laws of good husbandry, maintain rotations and carry out thorough cultivation to build up soil fertility. Of course, farmers have to strive for maximum profitability and survival, but increasingly from the end of the war, in 1945, there has been far too much exploitation of the land and of animals. Unacceptable practices such as battery hens, broilers, intensive veal and intensive pig production, are totally unnatural and give the livestock no opportunity for enjoyment. Anyone who has seen a lamb skipping in the sunshine or piglets chasing each other in the mud would understand what I mean.

Animals should be slaughtered in abattoirs as near as possible to the farm and transported chilled. Animals suffer greatly when crowded into trucks for long journeys abroad, often for fifty hours or more without rest or food or water, terrified and in extreme discomfort. It is callous lack of caring combined with profit as the main consideration that causes the horrendous and unnecessary cruelty to millions of animals a year. The British Government, like all European nations, can hide behind EEC regulations and World Trade Organisation rules, but if animals had votes Governments would very soon find a way of banning live exports. Organisations such as CIWF in the UK and similar organisations in Europe are doing splendid work in drawing attention to the appalling cruelty of live exports and they have achieved the eventual banning of battery hens. A number of show business personalities including Joanna Lumley and Brigitte Bardot are dedicated in their support for the animal cause.

It is quite a thought that each one of us, not only farmers, is given the task of continuing the work of creation and every day you and I are having an influence on the improvement or destruction of part of creation. We are all God's stewards and we have the opportunity and the responsibility of being involved in the healing process.

So now we turn to the healing of creation and again to St Francis. Above all, Francis loved God. He knew, as we know, that God first loved us. Francis responded to that love by giving himself in abject humility in God's service. He withdrew, like our Lord, for long periods of prayer and communion with God, an example that many have followed. The Franciscan Order grew rapidly, not by advertising or by offering an easy life – just the opposite. It grew through the example set by Francis of living close to God. In penitence we must pray for forgiveness for what we have done to creation, we must pray for guidance and for the necessary strength to heal the wounds. By example and by speaking out, we must bring others to help in the healing process. As with so many of today's troubles, a fundamental problem is that so many people do not believe in the existence of God. By grace, very many people do have a deep faith in the living God, and have experienced the power of prayer. Like Francis, if we love God, we must also love His creation and respect it, not abuse it. There are both Catholic and Anglican societies for the welfare of animals, and church services and retreats are held and excellent papers are given by experts. On one occasion we voted unanimously to petition the leaders of the nation's churches to take action to bring about the abolition of live exports. This was not granted, but I received a supportive telephone call from the Bishop of Dover, representing the Archbishop of Canterbury's diocese, who had himself been protesting on the picket line against live exports.

Farming is a partnership between the farmer, his co-workers and the Almighty. Men till the soil and sow the seed; God provides the rain and the climate for growth and increases the planted seed a hundred-fold and more in His great bounty. He has no hands but our hands and it is not enough merely to pray and leave it to Him – we have to get to work ourselves and do our bit for the healing of the land and to encourage others. May we have the guidance, the wisdom and the tenacity to fulfil our stewardship.

The Spark of God

We who believe in the sanctity of creation must act accordingly, nurture and cherish it and heal the wounds, glorifying God with all the angels, archangels and the whole company of Heaven, saying: 'Holy Holy Holy, Lord God of Hosts, Heaven and earth are full of thy glory, glory be to thee, O Lord most high.' Amen.

Chapter 15

FEEDING THE FLAME

I had assembled a great sheaf of notes and papers in preparation for writing this chapter. Everything fell on the floor and the first thing I picked up was a small piece of paper dated 19th June 1999 5.20 a.m., containing the words below:

GOD'S LOVE – PRESENCE – GLORY
PREPARATION – SACRIFICE AND DEDICATION

POWER IN HIS NAME – SERVICE – PERSISTENCE
IN PRAYER – OPENNESS – HUMILITY ALWAYS

Each of us has their own particular image of God, in accordance with family background and teaching and our own experience of God and of time spent with Him – in private or in worship. If we really want the relationship to deepen and become more meaningful it will do.

Five twenty a.m. is a good time for thoughts on God and I would not want to change any of that. It might be worth spending a little time reflecting on each of those lines. Those first words, God's LOVE, PRESENCE, GLORY happen to be the source of my own flame, the three awarenesses of God that I was given that evening in Wales in 1958 – His love pouring in, then awareness of His presence, finally, as I fell to my knees, being flooded with His glory. Understandably, this made an extremely deep and lasting impression on me, deepened my commitment to God and virtually changed faith to certainty. My spark was truly ignited. Yet I did not shout it from the housetops; for a long time I felt unable to tell the details even to my wife. Today, over forty years on, I would only mention it if I felt led to do so, in order to help someone to increase their faith. Understandably, most people who have not received a similar experience do not want to know, but they may well have received other gifts, perhaps less dramatic, but of even greater significance to them. 'Knowledge is more important than experiences' a priest once said to me, and for some that must be so and we are all different. We have different works to do for the Lord, making use of whatever gifts He has given us. Whatever gifts He gives, they are for use humbly in His service, to His glory.

We need to work together, support one another, and put to constructive service the energy we waste in criticising others. 'First pull the plank out of your own eye before removing a speck from your brother's eye.' How true and practical our Lord's teaching is! Why do we (and I do include me) not make greater efforts rigidly to follow and obey His teaching? A good Lent resolution would be to try harder to do so. We can only be fully effective if we live as closely as possible to Jesus in His example and His teaching.

I am assuming that, by this stage of the book, only the followers of Jesus are still with me, though it would be wonderful to think that one from outside the fold had come in with us. Co-workers, how can we help forward the cause of Christ? There is much work to be done and many of you will already be carrying a heavy load. We are all aware of splendid human beings, dutiful, kind and compassionate, who have not received the gift of faith and who do not have a relationship with Almighty God as a practising Christian. Their spark is not yet ignited. In many ways they may be better, kinder human beings than many of us committed Christians; they do belong within the fold. How do we bring them in? All that is needed is for these people to become aware of the reality of the love and power of God and to be open to Him. Words will not do it. To pray privately without the person being aware is a proven way and the best I know in such cases.

Of course, it is not only the good whom we must seek to enrol. However badly anyone may have behaved in the past, if they are truly repentant and are open about their condition and try to comply, then membership and all the benefits are granted. Even if anyone breaks the rules, provided they confess and try to go straight, they will be re-admitted to membership of the Church. If rules are broken, the member must be open and make confession of any lapses and ask for help in keeping free from this problem in future. We know that if this is done in sincerity, complete remission is granted and there is no troubled conscience. Confession and absolution as formal rites mainly apply to the Roman Catholic and Anglo-Catholic Churches but appropriate informal ministry should be available in any church community.

Christians are up against the scepticism of the materialist world and, as in the parable of the sower: the 'worldly cares and the false glamour of wealth'. Rooted solely in materialism many of those who do not believe in God appear not to believe either in the powers of evil. These always have been a reality. Fundamentally vanquished, the powers of Satan still lurk, ready to take advantage of a moment of weakness. Likewise, just as there are blessings, so from the devil there are curses, including curses that have been inflicted on succeeding generations of certain families. Curses can always be dealt with through a specialised ministry in the sacred name of Jesus, but, like exorcism, only by trained and approved ministers. In the hands of amateurs, things can go very wrong.

I thoroughly recommend a fascinating and most helpful book by Dr Kenneth McAll, *Healing The Family Tree*. Based on this book, our chaplain Pat Ashe led a service for the healing of our family through the generations and it was something that we were all glad to have done. I have attended similar services for other families. Such things as stillbirths, abortions, hauntings, burials at sea and any unknown spiritual problems in past generations can be covered.

I mentioned earlier the importance of not criticising or judging fellow Christians. I do admit to being irritated by Christians who state that there is no such thing as luck. I was even chided because one of our videos had ended with the words: '. . . and Good Luck.' Luck is a fact of life. God does not arrange for people to be on an aircraft when it crashes or in a building blown-up by terrorists and He certainly does not decide which person wins the lottery jackpot. If God were in control of everything, we should be merely His robots, with no free will. The existence of luck is part of the answer to people who say: 'I cannot believe in a God who allows suffering.' We could just leave it at that, but the next question must be: 'If God does not control these things, what is the use of praying?' As Christians, we have faith and we pray. Indeed, our Lord told us to pray.

I should again emphasise that in this book I am sharing my personal thoughts, which are not necessarily the edicts of the faith and you may be better informed. As I see it, God does not organise the traffic system, but He can and does guide us if we pray and makes us extra alert at times of danger. He does not control our lives, but He loves us and He has compassion.

Sue and I will never forget a seemingly miraculous avoidance of an accident, when along with his wife we were being driven by our friend, a retired doctor in his late eighties. Suddenly a youth in a car drove straight across our path on a sea-front road. We all felt a collision inevitable. Yet, somehow, our friend managed to stop in time. It was dramatic. Of course we congratulated the driver and his response was: 'I always pray before setting out on any journey.' There must be many similar examples where prayer has led to guidance, discernment or calm as well as, sometimes, a bigger miracle.

God does not prevent us from getting ill and I have known monks who suffered from cancer and died, but they died well. The prayers of believers are never in vain and in our Christian Cancer Group we can testify to the transformation of many patients who lived and died in awareness of God and at peace. It is also a fact that every day people are being miraculously healed through prayer.

Although God allows us free will and does not control our actions, we know that He does love us and if we pray He will guide us, support us and empower us in His service. For those who say: 'I cannot accept a God who allows suffering' or 'Why should the good die young?', my answer is that the world we are in today represents the 'nursery slopes' for the glories of the life to come. Those who are deaf to everything beyond the realities of this mortal life doubtless pity the naivety of those who believe. But it is the non-believers who are missing out and it is a great joy that, as in the time of Acts, 'more are added to the believers day by day.'

Our present society wants to know and understand before being prepared to accept anything. But God is sublime, beyond our understanding. The only thing we need to know is that God is perfect love, love that has been prepared to suffer torture, humiliation and death for us through Christ Jesus. That love is waiting to be poured in to give us awareness, discernment, power and spiritual gifts, to be used in God's service and to His glory.

As for the life to come, of course, you and I can only

225

guess at the joys of Heaven. It must be very special, for we know that already there are the angels, the archangels, the saints and martyrs through the centuries and the whole company of Heaven. We worship God and try to do His will because we love Him, not in order to qualify for admission. Nevertheless, it helps to have the promise of eternal life and 'Peace at the last'.

Having shared these thoughts with you I would like to have a short interlude to quote, with his permission, that great man Archbishop Donald Coggan ('The Great Opportunity' from *Sure Foundation*, Hodder, out of print) on the subject of evangelism. Archbishop Coggan preached at the dedication of the great doors of St Paul's-within-the-Walls Anglican Church in Rome. He took as his text 1 Corinthians 16:9 'A great opportunity has opened for effective work, and there is much opposition.' The archbishop went on to explain the context. St Paul was working at Ephesus where there was considerable opposition and he was also planning a journey to Corinth where the Church had been established in the face of hostility. Despite the problems, the work of evangelism, the preaching of the gospel . . . must go on, not in spite of the difficulties but because of them. In the archbishop's words:

> The world to which the Christian Church goes in the twentieth century is not unlike that to which the Church went in the first. Vast multitudes even today have never heard the name of Jesus. Many . . . where Christianity has existed for centuries, only know that name as a swear word; and others among them know so little of Him as to make no sense of His religion. In the West there is a widespread disillusion with politics and, among the more thoughtful, with materialism, as in the first century there was disillusion with the 'Gods many and Laws many', whose images were seen in every city

and town. Their world was rightly described by St Paul as 'without God and without hope'. That would be a fair description of a large part of our world. The sheer sense of disillusion constitutes for the Christian 'a great door', 'a great opportunity for effective work' . . . Opposition? Yes – in plenty. But that is no cause for hesitation. Rather is it a summons to action.

What a rallying call! We do live in times of real opportunity; seeing all too clearly signs of decadence, the breakdown of standards and morality, all the evils of selfish materialism and the resulting divorces, drink, drugs, single-parent families etc. Yes, we know all that, we read it daily in the papers, we see it on TV. This is an age of spin-doctors, truth-benders and glib tongues; you are left behind if you are not on the Internet and, if you cry 'shame', you are square and not with it. God is mocked. His commandments, His teaching, are ignored. The question is: 'What can we do?' Remember Donald Coggan: 'Without God and without hope'. So it is a time of opportunity. I believe that an increasing number of people are realising that we cannot go on as we are and we must get on to sound foundations. The only way ahead is through Almighty God.

Of course, it would be wrong to give the impression that no one is any good. There are millions of wonderful people and we have got to work to bring in more and more of them to faith. Each one of us can do something and many individual Christians and groups are being led into new initiatives, often making use of their own resources in terms of homes or buildings, as well as giving time and money for Christian purposes. Some initiatives are based on a particular church but most are non-denominational and available to all. Most of the population are not churchgoers, and experience proves that people who have never been to church or who have 'dropped-out' are more likely to be brought in through activities that do not take place in church.

There is nothing new in individuals being led to create initiatives for God. From earliest Christian times there have been individuals and groups of dedicated Christians praying, teaching, preaching, and helping the sick and the poor. These have included the great Christian Orders founded by St Francis, St Benedict and many others. Nearly all began with an individual and formal recognition by Rome came later. Today's initiators are also people of prayer, open to God's leading and seeking to serve Him and to bring others to awareness of His love.

There seems to be a growing feeling that it is inappropriate to differentiate between Christian and non-Christian ministry, counselling and other facilities. Increasingly, the boundaries between holy and holistic are becoming fogged. There are fundamental differences. In the care sector in general it strikes me that the official attitude is something like this: 'It is accepted that there are some people who still believe in God, but the majority now accept that God is dead and we have to get on with our modern therapies. We don't want people talking about God, it is embarrassing.' This is not a case of 'Without God, without hope' but 'Without God but with bags of technology and much that is good.' Yet something vital is lacking.

There is a depth and a peace that goes with true Christian ministry and counselling, which cannot be matched by the secular. Who but the Christian can offer hope to the dying? Many voluntary and professional care workers are Christians. They obviously have to be sensitive about this and to be prepared to make known their Christian faith only when appropriate. It was generally accepted that most people when ill appreciated prayer, but when the leader of a self-help Cancer Group phoned and asked for 'healers', I replied that we had no 'healers' but we would be pleased to come and pray. 'Oh no, they'll think that they are dying if you start praying!' I hope that that is not typical, but he was the leader of a caring, holistic group. It is always a joy when visiting sick people in hospital to be able to quietly – often silently – pray with them. Prayer is positive and sustaining, whereas for the very ill talk can be draining.

There are many Christian initiatives in private homes, some of which have been operating for several decades, including Ashburnham House in Sussex and Trelowaren in Cornwall. Burrswood Christian Home of Healing in Kent, founded in 1948 by Dorothy Kerin, is another fine example mentioned elsewhere. A more recent Christian Centre closely linked to the ministry of healing is Harnhill near Cirencester. This was the vision of a retired Canon, Arthur Dodds, for the use of a farmhouse and adjoining buildings on the retirement of his friends Robert and Mary Henley. The adjoining gem of a little church made this particularly auspicious and with the support of the prayerful community, Harnhill continues to develop strongly as a centre of Christian healing, teaching and evangelism. Over the past twelve years the builders have been constantly coming and going, extending, building, converting, and always improving facilities without spoiling the lovely site. There are two healing services each week, with up to one hundred people in the barn on Wednesday evenings, and seventy in the church for a Friday morning Communion Service.

There must be tens of thousands of Christian initiatives in people's houses, including Study Groups, Prayer Groups and Healing Prayer Groups. Many of these are linked to their own churches; others are non-denominational. Not all groups are directly under the control of a parish but it is essential that the group is properly constituted and run by responsible Christians. Any individual or group wishing to minister Christian healing should not do so without sanction either from the parish, diocese or a national body such as the Acorn Christian Healing Trust.

Some of the most effective initiatives come from people who have suffered from problems and found no one to turn to. A Christian mother whose five-month-old baby developed cancer, and happily recovered, has formed a thriving national Christian organisation for parents of children with cancer. On the day that we first met her we were also visited by two Christian ladies from a Sheffield hospital, a doctor and an ordained radiologist who were proposing to form a Christian support group for their cancer patients. Most of the wonderful hospices have been initiated and funded by local people.

Following a pilgrimage to Medjugorje, a Surrey landowner and his wife had the vision to create a 'Pilgrimage of Stations of the Cross' over a half-mile scenic route at Wintershall, Bramley, Surrey. This has been splendidly accomplished, starting at a little Franciscan chapel by a lake and ending on top of a hill with breathtaking views where a larger chapel has been built in which the stained-glass window of the resurrection represents the final Station of the Cross. The pilgrimage is available to all, at 7 a.m. on the first Friday of each month. It is led by ordained ministers or monks of any denomination. Special services are also held during the year in the barn at the top of the hill. The Wintershall Passion Play and the Life of Christ are now established in the calendar and people flock to see them from all parts of the British Isles and even from overseas. Peter and Anne Hutley are comparatively new active Christians, originally Anglicans but both now accepted into the Roman Catholic Church. Their work has been recognised by a well-deserved Templeton Award, presented by the Dean of Windsor at a special ceremony. Wintershall is certainly making an outstanding contribution to putting God on the map, not only in Surrey. We do have many more initiatives in the area, including a retired diplomat, Sir John Ford, who writes and publishes Christian books and puts them on the Internet.

The national charity 'Christian Outreach' began as 'Project Vietnamese Orphans' when Marion Ashe, the vicar's wife, heard on the radio the news of vast numbers of Vietnamese orphans desperately needing homes. The men's group were meeting in the rectory at the time and Marion told them the news when serving the coffee. The immediate reaction was 'Let's try to rescue one'. From that small beginning a long, very difficult and dramatically successful operation ensued, a charity was founded and others followed. Pat Ashe and his team, being a relatively small operation, managed to gain entry into important headquarters in Vietnam that were barred to the bigger organisations. There are times when 'small is beautiful'. We were fortunate to have Pat and Marion living near us in retirement and to have Pat as our Chaplain at Loseley and Littleton.

Under the auspices and encouragement of the Acorn Christian Healing Trust, several local initiatives have been set up in family homes by individuals and groups in various parts of the country. These include Christian cancer help centres, a Christian listener and quiet day centre, initiatives for the mentally sick, a drop-in centre, counselling, as well as doctor/clergy groups and day centres and homes for elderly people.

Mothers' Prayers is a programme recently formed for mothers who wish to pray together for their children and grandchildren. Sandra, a young mother, had been awakened in the night with the words: 'Pray for your children.' This happened on two occasions. This led Sandra and her sister-in-law Veronica to pray regularly for their children and they then met with three other mothers. This spread rapidly and, after three years, spread to many countries throughout the world without any publicity having been initiated. Many blessings have been reported, including many children coming back to their faith and children coming home after long absences. One mother, after praying at her very first meeting, was reconciled one week later with a daughter she had not seen for seven years. In Chapter 13 I mentioned the practice of seeking guidance through opening the Bible at random. Veronica, one of the founders of Mothers' Prayers did this when seeking guidance. The Bible opened at Jeremiah 31:16–17:

> These are the words of the LORD to her:
> Cease your weeping,
> shed no more tears;
> for there will be a reward for your toil,
> and they will return from the enemy's land.
> There will be hope for your posterity;
> your children will return within their own borders.

I mention these few of the innumerable Christian initiatives to make the point that there is a flood of ideas, energy and great resources in buildings, land and facilities still waiting to be used in spreading the Christian message and bringing care and love to people in need. Such ventures bring great blessings and fulfilment for those involved and provide for the Christian cause far greater resources than the churches alone could muster. But they must be undertaken prayerfully, seeking God's guidance and in humility.

Is God 'doing a new thing'? Not new perhaps, for the Holy Spirit has always been leading individuals to new initiatives, but in this age it does seem either that there are more promptings and leadings, or perhaps Christians are becoming more responsive – probably both. The potential is unlimited and carries the seeds of a real movement back to God. Churches need to encourage and support appropriate initiatives and not feel threatened by them, as does happen. We could, of course, call our Christian Cancer Health

Centre by the name of St Nicholas Church, Compton. This would not be appropriate because we draw our patients from a forty-mile radius and they are not all Anglicans and not all church people. Nevertheless, because we call ourselves Loseley, some church people may have kept away, feeling that we were 'doing our own thing'. We do give an open invitation to clergy of all denominations to come and see and, better still, to bring one of their cancer patients. The invitation always remains open but, sadly, few of our patients get led to us by their churches.

Last, but certainly not least, must come Alpha. Most people by now know of the Alpha Christian training courses, introduced by Holy Trinity Church, Brompton. Year by year more and more people are enrolling on the courses. In 1999 over 1.5 million people in all the major denominations in ninety-six countries took the twelve-week course. In the words of the organisers: 'It explores faith in new and stimulating ways. Applicable for both people with no Christian background, as well as for ordinary parishioners, leading to a personal encounter with the living Jesus Christ.' There should be an Alpha course near you. The mix of parishioners with people from outside the churches, talking openly about faith and disbelief, is in itself constructive but there is plenty of positive teaching which is also the subject of discussion. The courses take place on one evening a week, always commencing with supper. A further exciting fact is that the same Alpha courses are run by all main denominations: I have attended part of an RC Alpha course, using the same videos and printed material as Anglican Alphas.

With all the varied Christian initiatives afoot, there is no longer the excuse for anyone to be put off religion because of the local parson or the atmosphere of the church building. Christianity is alive, not something confined to a building or to a particular ordained person. In this book I have included many reasons for believing in the existence of God – Father, Son and Holy Spirit. In the light of my own experience, I regard God as fact. Particularly at times of serious illness and the approach of death, faith in God is the most important gift of all. The sense of peace and sometimes even joy experienced by dying Christians contrasts starkly with the unbelievers' resentment, helplessness and often fear. When we discover Almighty God we feel the need to worship Him and because we love Him, we need to serve Him and make Him better known and loved.

After I had embarked on writing this book, I was away from home and walking past a very small Catholic church. I felt the urge to go in for a minute and my eye was taken by one of the cards for sale on the little table. It read:

'God give me work till my life shall end
And life till my work is done.'

I am not usually one for texts, but I really identified the last line with the writing of this book. I did want to live to finish it and to complete my testimony, however onerous it might be. Now at last I lay down my pen, pass on The Spark and feel at peace. Thanks be to God.

APPENDIX 1

References to the Holy Spirit in Acts and the Epistles

Acts 1:8	'But you will receive power when the Holy Spirit comes upon you; and you will bear witness for me in Jerusalem . . .'
Acts 2:4	They were all filled with the Holy Spirit and began to talk in other tongues, as the Spirit gave them power of utterance.
Acts 4:31	When they had ended their prayer, the building where they were assembled rocked, and all were filled with the Holy Spirit and spoke God's word with boldness.
Acts 5:32	'. . . And we are witnesses to all this, as is the Holy Spirit who is given by God to those obedient to Him.'
Acts 6:3,5	'Therefore, friends, pick seven men of good repute from your number, men full of the Spirit and of wisdom . . .' They elected Stephen, a man full of faith and of the Holy Spirit . . .
Acts 7:55	But Stephen, filled with the Holy Spirit, and gazing intently up to Heaven, saw the glory of God and Jesus standing at God's right hand.
Acts 10:38,44	'You know how God anointed Jesus of Nazareth with the Holy Spirit and with power . . .' Peter was still speaking when the Holy Spirit came upon all who were listening to the message.
Acts 11:15	'Hardly had I begun speaking, when the Holy Spirit came upon them, just as upon us at the beginning, and I recalled what the Lord had said: "John baptized with water, but you will be baptized with the Holy Spirit."'
Acts 13:2	While they were offering worship to the Lord and fasting, the Holy Spirit said:, 'Set Barnabas and Saul apart for me, to do the work to which I have called them.'
Acts 13:9	But Saul, also known as Paul, filled with the Holy Spirit, fixed his eyes on him and said, 'You are a swindler, an out-and-out fraud! . . .'
Acts 13:52	And the disciples were filled with joy and with the Holy Spirit.
Acts 15:8	'And God, who can read human hearts, showed His approval

	by giving the Holy Spirit to them as He did to us.'
Acts 15:28	'It is the decision of the Holy Spirit, and our decision, to lay no further burden upon you beyond these essentials . . .'
Acts 16:6	They travelled through the Phrygian and Galatian region, prevented by the Holy Spirit from delivering the message in the province of Asia. When they approached the Mysian border they tried to enter Bithynia, but, as the Spirit of Jesus would not allow them, they passed . . .
Acts 19:2,6	When he asked them, 'Did you receive the Holy Spirit when you became believers?' they replied, 'No, we were not even told that there is a Holy Spirit.' . . . when Paul laid his hands on them, the Holy Spirit came upon them and they spoke in tongues of ecstasy and prophesied.
Acts 20:23	'. . . in city after city the Holy Spirit assures me that imprisonment and hardships await me.'
Acts 21:11	[Agabus] came to us, took Paul's belt, bound his own feet and hands with it, and said, 'These are the words of the Holy Spirit: Thus will the Jews in Jerusalem bind the man to whom this belt belongs, and hand him over to the Gentiles.'
Rom 5:5	. . . through the Holy Spirit He has given us, God's love has flooded our hearts.
Rom 14:17	. . . for the kingdom of God is not eating and drinking, but justice, peace, and joy, inspired by the Holy Spirit.
1 Cor. 2:13	. . . and, because we are interpreting spiritual truths to those who have the Spirit, we speak of these gifts of God in words taught us not by our human wisdom but by the Spirit.
1 Cor 6:19	Do you not know that your body is a temple of the indwelling Holy Spirit, and the Spirit is God's gift to you?
2 Cor 13:14	The grace of the Lord Jesus Christ, and the love of God, and the fellowship of the Holy Spirit, be with you all.
Eph 4:7	But each of us has been given a special gift, a particular share in the bounty of Christ. . . . And it is He who has given some to be apostles, some prophets, some evangelists, some pastors and teachers, to equip God's people for work in His service, for the building up of the body of Christ.
1 Thess 1:5	. . . when we brought you the gospel we did not bring it in mere words but in the power of the Holy Spirit . . .
1 Thess 1:6	. . . the welcome you gave the message meant grave suffering for you, yet you rejoiced in the Holy Spirit . . .

APPENDIX 2

Some Centres of Christian Healing and Training
(It is advisable to check details by phone before travelling)

ACORN CHRISTIAN HEALING TRUST
Whitehill Chase, High Street, Bordon, Hants, GU35 0AP. Tel: 01420 478121
Short courses including Christian Listening; Annual Conference (details on application). Healing service every Tuesday at noon.

BURRSWOOD CHRISTIAN COMMUNITY (founded by Dorothy Kerin)
Groombridge, Tunbridge Wells, Kent, TN3 9PY. Tel: 01892 863637
Guesthouse, 35-bed medical centre, hydrotherapy pool, chapels. Weekly healing service 11.30 a.m. Thursday. Church of Christ the Healer. The mission – To heal the sick, comfort the sorrowing and give faith to the faithless; to provide Christian healthcare to those who would benefit, regardless of financial status; to keep the love of Christ at the heart of care and to be a sign of the kingdom of God. Residential Christian caring and ministry. Lovely grounds.

CROWHURST CHRISTIAN HEALING CENTRE
The Old Rectory, Crowhurst, Battle, East Sussex, TN33 9AD. Tel: 01424 830204
Healing ministry and services. Guests up to two weeks. Courses on healing ministry.

THE HARNHILL CENTRE OF CHRISTIAN HEALING

The Spark of God

Harnhill Manor, Cirencester, GL7 5PX. Tel: 01285 850283
There are many courses and lectures throughout the year. The ministry is prayer-based; details on application.
Services: Wednesday (barn) 7.30 p.m., Fridays 10.30 a.m. service and Communion in church.

GREEN PASTURES CHRISTIAN CENTRE OF HEALING

17 Burton Road, Branksome Park, Poole, Dorset, BH13 6DT. Tel: 01202 764776
Residential Christian centre. Daily prayer and worship in chapel with opportunity for prayer for healing. Counselling and retreats. Spiritual direction by special arrangement.

CARISBROOKE PRIORY TRUST

39 Whitcombe Road, Newport, Isle of Wight, PO30 1YS. Tel: 01983 523354
This centre is in its early stages of development. Services are held on Thursdays from 12 noon–1 p.m., with opportunity for prayer for healing, followed by lunch and afternoon optional activities. Bible study, art, craft and relaxation. Training and Christian listening and psychotherapy are offered and there are quiet days and opportunities to help in house and garden. Further details on request.

APPENDIX 3

Further reading

The Bible
> '*The Bible has a reassuring everlastingness which allows it to speak with equal effort to every Age . . . It is, after all, the Word of God.*' John Dalrymple

The following provide more detailed information on subjects included, in alphabetical order.

A Healing House of Prayer, Morris Maddocks (Guildford: Eagle).

Angels, Hope Price (London: Macmillan).

Dorothy Kerin, As I Knew Her, Marina Chavchavadze (executors of author).

Healing the Family Tree, Kenneth McAll (London: Sheldon Press).

Holiness, Donald Nicholl (London: Darton, Longman & Todd).

Listening, Anne Long (London: Daybreak).

Miracles, Geoff Hope Price (London: Macmillan).

Nine O'Clock in the Morning, Dennis and Rita Bennett (Eastbourne: Kingsway).

St Francis of Assisi

Simple Prayer, John Dalrymple (London: Darton, Longman & Todd).

The Christian Healing Ministry, Morris Maddocks (London: SPCK).

The Heart of Healing, George Bennett (Evesham: Arthur James).

The Prayer That Heals, Francis MacNutt (London: Hodder & Stoughton).

The Genesse Diary, Henri J. Nouwen (New York: Doubleday).

The Servant Son, Donald Coggan (London: SPCK).

To Be a Pilgrim, Basil Hume OSB (London: SPCK).

Where Is the Winning Post?, Phil Shirley (London: HarperCollins).

You Are My God, David Watson (London: Hodder & Stoughton).